Answering the Contemplative Call

First Steps on the Mystical Path

CARL McCOLMAN

HAMPTON ROADS

Cover design by *www.levanfisherdesign.com*/Barbara Fisher
Cover art by *Mel Curtis*/*photodisc*/*getty images*
Text design by Dutton & Sherman Design

Hampton Roads Publishing Company, Inc.
Charlottesville, VA 22906
Distributed by Red Wheel/Weiser, LLC

Unless noted otherwise, scripture quotations are from the New Revised Standard
Version Bible, © 1989, Division of Christian Education of the National Council of
Churches of Christ in the United States of America. Used by permission. All Rights
Reserved.

ISBN 978-1-57174-677-1

Praise for *Answering the Contemplative Call*

"It is not often that a book is both very practical and very inspiring at the same time. Carl McColman gives you much wise direction and broad understanding of the field of contemplative theory and practice. The need is too great today to waste time relearning what has already been learned—so well. Here is your teacher!"

—Fr. Richard Rohr, O.F.M.
Center for Action and Contemplation, Albuquerque, New Mexico

". . . a magnificent primer on contemplative spirituality . . . a first rate contribution to the conversation about the vital relevance of ancient spiritual practices for contemporary people thirsting for communion with God."

—Ian Morgan Cron, author of *Jesus, My Father, the CIA, and Me: A Memoir of Sorts* and *Chasing Francis: A Pilgrim's Tale*

". . . Carl McColman creates a safe and beautiful space where each of us can come—human as we are—and learn how possible it is to befriend silence and to live in the certain joy of daily intimacy with God."

— Carmen Acevedo Butcher, translator of *The Cloud of Unknowing* and author of *Man of Blessing: A Life of St. Benedict*

". . . invites us on a journey of love where everyone is welcome and worthy, and it is impossible to get lost. It is a journey that necessarily begins within, and leads ever-deeper inward, to a place of resonant silence. Bountiful quotes from mystics who have walked the path before us provide a series of luminous stepping-stones for own adventure."

— Mirabai Starr, author of *God of Love: A Guide to the Heart of Judaism, Christianity and Islam*

"Carl McColman masterfully maps out for the serious spiritual seeker the nature of the mystical experience and outlines a clear and accessible pathway on how to get there."

—Kyriacos C. Markides, author of *The Mountain of Silence* and *Inner River*

For Fran, my lovely wife, my dearest friend, my partner in contemplation, and my companion on the journey of kenosis.

To You, silence is praise, O God in Zion; and unto You shall the vow be fulfilled.

—Psalm 65:2, Stone Edition Tanach[1]

Contents

Part One

Recognizing the Call

Part Two

Preparing for the Journey

Part Three

Embarking on the Adventure

Acknowledgments

Writing a book is, in many ways, like other elements of Christian spirituality: it entails a dynamic balance between solitude and community. Along with the many hours spent toiling away by myself with only my trusty computer (and a few cats) for companionship, I have relied on friends, colleagues, and brothers and sisters in the faith for support, nurture, challenge, and insight.

Greg Brandenburgh and Linda Roghaar, thank you both so much for your support, guidance, and honesty. Everyone at Hampton Roads and Red Wheel/Weiser has been most helpful. The monks, Lay Cistercians, employees, and friends of the Monastery of the Holy Spirit continue to be a blessing in so many ways. While listing just a few people is problematic because so many of you deserve my thanks, I feel I must particularly mention Fr. Anthony Delisi, Fr. Tom Francis Smith, Br. Elias Marechal, Br. Cassian Russell, Linda Mitchell, Paco and Malika Ambrosetti, Rocky Thomas, and Michael Thompson for your friendship, guidance, and encouragement.

Other friends and colleagues whose support has been invaluable include Rick Branaman, Andy Fitz-Gibbon, Phil Foster, Dana Greene, Darrell Grizzle, Gareth Higgins, Ben Campbell Johnson, Brian D. McLaren, Michael Morrell, Edd Salazar SJ, Ann Temkin, and Karen Davis Young.

I am haunted by the thought that I have forgotten someone. If I have, I can only trust that you know who you are and you know my heart knows gratitude beyond the frailties of my imperfect memory. Finally, my deepest gratitude continues to flow toward my wife, Fran, and daughter, Rhiannon, who remain my closest friends, dearest companions, and living sacraments, through their love, of God's grace in my life. Words simply cannot express how much I cherish you and am grateful for you.

Introduction

"All the world's a stage," said William Shakespeare, "and all the men and women merely players." This metaphor—seeing the human experience in terms of the stories we tell and the masks we wear—is a natural one for a playwright to use. A few centuries later, the game inventor Milton Bradley offered a different way of thinking about the world: as a game. His Game of Life was one of the most popular parlor games of the nineteenth century, and a revised version of it remains on the market today.

Long before the days when actors thrilled audiences in the Globe Theatre, however, or families laughed as they playfully competed to move their tokens across a board, writers and mystics and other spiritual seekers used another metaphor to describe the adventure of life— a journey. Consider two of the great works of literature of the Middle Ages—Geoffrey Chaucer's *Canterbury Tales* and Dante's *Divine Comedy*. Chaucer compares the human experience to a religious pilgrimage, while Dante offers a multilayered look at the cosmology of his day, as his literary self travels from hell to purgatory to heaven. "Life is a journey," declared the eighteenth century writer Oliver Goldsmith, adding this little bit of Irish humor: "a journey that must be traveled no matter how bad the roads and accommodations." Almost as a response to Goldsmith's sarcasm, Ralph Waldo Emerson linked the journey motif to the spiritual quest when he said: "What lies behind us and what lies before us are tiny matters compared to what lies within us."

Among the mystics of the Christian tradition, this journey metaphor crops up again and again, in a variety of ways—not only in the idea of traveling long distances, but in even more humble imagery like running a race, climbing a ladder, or exploring a castle. Early contemplatives loved the story of Moses and the Hebrew people wandering for years in the desert before finding their home in the Promised Land. In the fourth century, Saint Gregory of Nyssa wrote *The Life of Moses*, using elements from the Exodus story to explain the beauty and mystery of Christian spirituality. A century and a half later, Saint Benedict compared the monastic life to running a race. Guigo II, in the twelfth century, used the image of climbing a ladder to explain the spirituality of sacred reading. Walter Hilton (fourteenth century) revisited the ladder (or stairway) motif, while in the sixteenth century, Saint John of the Cross likened the mystical path to *The Ascent of Mount Carmel* and his comrade Teresa of Avila wrote about exploring *The Interior Castle*. Even in the twentieth century, the Trappist contemplative Thomas Merton borrowed a page from Dante and called his autobiography *The Seven Storey Mountain*, while the Irish poet and spiritual author John O'Donohue played the contrarian and insisted: "If there were a spiritual journey, it would be only a quarter inch long"! He went on to tip his hat to Emerson, noting that "the eternal is at home—within you."[2]

So if life is a journey, then spirituality is an essential part of the passage. Mysticism is not some sort of static experience, a moment in time in which a person feels especially united with God. Rather, it is a process, an unfolding dimension of movement and change that takes place over the course of many seasons. Emerson and O'Donohue are

Answering the Contemplative Call

right, of course: this journey is in large measure an inner trek, a quest to find the mysteries at the heart of the universe, paradoxically nestled within the heart of your own soul. I don't think I'll be giving away too much too soon to mention that this journey is, in fact, riddled with paradox. The destination that mystics seek is precisely where they begin their quest. The goal of the journey is, at least in part, to have no goal; the purpose is not so much to find God as to find ourselves in God. We can devote years to the quest only to find that, after all that time, we are still at the beginning of the route. These are just a few of the twists and switchbacks that we may encounter along the way. But those who have embarked on this pilgrimage soon realize that each paradox is part of the beauty of the journey.

It is my distinct honor and privilege to invite you on this excursion. Of course, it is not really my place to do so—for I am merely another traveler, like you. My invitation is that of a friend calling out to a friend: "Hey, come along; this promises to be a fascinating adventure!"

Every journey begins at the beginning, and often that is months or even years before the first step is taken. Before my first trip overseas, I had already daydreamed about going for years, and then spent three months planning my itinerary prior to that fateful day I showed up at the Atlanta airport, quivering with excitement. Sometimes we may travel on the spur of the moment, or even under emergency circumstances, as when we rush home to attend to a dying relative. But there is always a beginning—a point at which the decision is made to embark on the voyage. These are the questions around which I have organized this book: What can we say about that decisive moment when a person makes a commitment to the spirituality of contemplation and the Christian mysteries? And once we have entered into that moment of decision, then what? What is involved in preparing for and launching our adventure, which promises to take us to the very heart of God?

Right away, I know words like *mysticism* or *mystical* or *contemplative* may be a challenge for some. These are not simple words that describe easy concepts; rather, they point to a rich and many-layered dimension of spirituality. Furthermore, they mean different things to different people. One person may speak of *mysticism* as a shorthand word for intimacy with God, while another may use the same word to refer to supernatural experiences, with no reference to God at all. At the risk of being overly simplistic, I'm using this word very much in the intimacy with God sense. As the Catholic social activist and writer Catherine De Hueck Doherty noted: "A mystic is simply a man or woman in love with God, and the Church is hungry for such people."[3]

What does she mean by the second part of that statement? Simply this: that the mystical life is a blessing not only for the person who enters it, but for the entire community of believers and spiritual seekers. Mystics are not only in love with God; they are also beacons of Divine love for everyone they meet (which includes not only other followers of Christ, but indeed *all* people).

Likewise, contemplation (as in contemplative prayer or the contemplative life) points to the love of God—at least in my understanding of the word. If a mystic is a lover of God, then contemplation is the means by which Divine love is given, received, and shared. *Contemplative prayer*, for example, is a term used in a variety of ways; it can refer to silent prayer, centering prayer, meditative prayer, and the prayer of the heart, etc. But what all these different shades of contemplation have in common is that they are all immersed in and infused with the love of God.

Like *mysticism*, *contemplation* is a universal word that can be used in a variety of contexts. I am writing as a member of the Christian tradition; so when I speak of mysticism and contemplation, I refer specifically to the Christian journey into the love of God. My way of explaining and interpreting the contemplative life, and the language I use to do so, are all shaped by Christianity's unique understanding of mystical wisdom. But I am trying to remember, humbly, that not everyone who reads this book will be Christian, and that many people who have had dealings with Christianity-the-institution have been wounded by the imperfect, human side of the religion. There is no way that I, as a writer, can effectively address so many different people with so many different spiritual needs, other than to share my own perspective on things, which is what I have tried to do. Beyond that, I must trust in the grace of God—and the forgiveness of my readers—if my way of explaining things is sometimes incomplete or less than artful.

For my readers who are engaged with the religious expression of Christianity, I hope this book represents an invitation to take your faith to a new and deeper level of intimacy with God. For those who have no connection with Christianity, or who have been wounded by the many imperfections found within the Church, I ask only that you keep an open mind as you read along. Perhaps the love of God will call out to you in a way that's right for you as well.

While I do not assume that my readers are necessarily Christian, or necessarily have a preexisting interest in mystical or contemplative spirituality, I *do* make one assumption about people who are likely to read a book like this. I assume that you have noticed a longing or yearning in your heart and soul—a desire for something more. It's not really something you can put into words, and you may never have shared this with anyone else. Even if your life is fairly rich with friends and loved ones and material abundance, you know that these treasures, precious as they are, do nothing to assuage this nameless yearning.

If you are a religious or spiritually minded person, you may identify that something more as God. Or perhaps you don't name it all, respecting how mysterious it is. That's fine. You may even have a sense that, if you explore this longing, the deeper you go, the more mysterious it gets. I'll take a closer look at this longing in the pages to come. For now, let's just say that it is the universal starting point for the mystical life. And if, by chance, you've picked up this book but *don't* have a sense of longing for that mysterious something more—at least not consciously—perhaps a lot of what I say in the pages to come won't make much sense to you. Of course, I invite you to read along anyway, if for no other reason than to get a sense of what inspires contemplatives—those who do feel that longing for something that just can't be put into words.

This book is organized into three sections. The first, "Recognizing the Call," begins with a simple idea that is central to Christian spirituality—that the gift of being loved by God (and even being able to love God in return) is just that: a gift. As the Carmelite writer Ruth Burrows puts it: "The mystical life is beyond our power, nothing we can do can bring it to us, but God is longing to give it to us, to all of us, not to a select few."[4] It is out of trust in that prevenient longing of God that I even dare to speak of the contemplative call. But out of that trust, I am confident that each one of us *is* called to the mystical life. The first part of the book explores what that may look like.

Part Two, "Preparing for the Journey," extends the travel metaphor to consider what we need to do in response to the contemplative call. At the risk of being overly whimsical, I use the metaphor to describe a variety of important tasks: getting a map, packing, and learning the language of the land where our trip will take us.

Finally, Part Three, "Embarking on the Adventure," considers what those first steps on the path (or the voyage) may look like. Please forgive me for playing rather loosely with my guiding metaphor; I explore the mystical life both as a path we walk and as a journey we travel. I think both metaphors are useful, and so I use both rather interchangeably. I ask my readers' forbearance in remembering that, pathway or journey, these words are simply symbolic ways of describing an interior alchemy that occurs in the human soul—the transformation from the normal human state of existential angst to serene recognition of the unifying presence of God.

In every chapter of the book, I quote one or more of the great mystics of the Christian tradition. I do this because part of the joy of

Answering the Contemplative Call

the mystical path is discovering the wisdom of the great contemplatives who have traveled along this way ahead of us. I think you will find that their words offer tremendous insight and encouragement for anyone who is seeking deeper intimacy with God.

I know that we are all at different points on our journeys, and while this book is particularly aimed at beginners, I hope that those whose spiritual journeys are well underway may find something useful here as well. As I mentioned above, part of the paradox of contemplation is that we are all, always, beginners. So no matter where you are on your adventure in the love of God, my prayer is that something in this book will be a blessing for you.

An Invitation

The "mystical path" is not simply an idea for our entertainment. It is a living tradition that extends as far back as humanity has been exploring the spiritual dimension of life. Mystical wisdom remains relevant for us alive today, and—I trust—will continue to bring light and understanding to generations yet unborn.

It is my honor as a writer, humble as my words may be, to invite you to explore the splendor of the mystical tradition with me. Thank you for reading! If you gain even a fraction of the insight and joy from the mystics that I have been blessed to receive, then I believe you will find the wisdom of the mystics to be a source of spiritual transformation and profound inner peace.

With this hope in mind, I invite you to join me, not merely in *reading* or *thinking* about the mystical life, but also in actually *engaging* with the wisdom of the mystics. There are many ways to do this—indeed, Part Three of the book is built on the idea that contemplation is not just a theory to be thought about, but is also a way of life to be practiced. For now, however, here are a few simple suggestions that can be helpful for anyone who seeks intimacy with God:

- Make an intentional effort to spend at least ten minutes every day in *silence*.

- Make an effort to *pray* in whatever way is comfortable for you at least once a day.

- Consider one area of your life that you want to *change:* perhaps you want to stop smoking, or clean out the attic, or begin volunteering one Saturday a month at your local homeless shelter. Whatever it is, decide on this one goal for self-improvement and try to do something every day—no matter how small or modest—to bring you closer to achieving your objective.

I know for some people, these goals may seem overly modest. Feel free to adjust them to your specific needs. If you already meditate daily for half an hour, see if you can stretch your commitment to forty minutes. The point behind these three suggestions is not that they will, in themselves, give you a radical spiritual makeover. Actually, the point is intentionally modest. These three exercises are meant to stretch you just a little bit, opening you up to the elusive presence of God through silence, prayer, and self-improvement.

You'll need to find the right balance of discipline to follow through on these tasks every day, but also a measure of humor and self-forgiveness for the inevitable times when you fail to live up to even these simple goals. Without the right measure of forgiveness, these invitations will rapidly morph into demanding chores. But without a basic commitment to discipline, you won't bother to explore these new practices at all.

Even though I'm only inviting you to change a small amount of your time and just one or two aspects of your life, if you do take me up on these three objectives, I suspect you will be pleasantly surprised at how they support the ideas found in this book—becoming closer to and more intimate with God. Intimacy with God is more than just

Answering the Contemplative Call

a nice thought. The mystics proclaim that this intimacy is available to all of us, but we do have to make the effort to receive the gift that is freely handed to us. Prayer, self-care, and attention to silence are all proven ways to dispose ourselves to receive the gift—the gifts—God is eager to give us. So, I invite you to take the risk: explore the beauty of Christian contemplation, not merely as an idea to ponder, but as a life to be lived.

A Note about Language

God transcends the human distinction between the sexes. He is nei-
ther man nor woman: he is God.

— Catechism of the Catholic Church, 239

One of the most controversial issues facing the Christian tradition today is the question of how we speak about God, especially in regard to gender. This issue is particularly thorny for writers.

The English language makes it difficult to express how God transcends the limitations of gender. Christian teaching insists that God is a *person*, not an *object*. For this reason, it is not appropriate to use gender-neutral pronouns like *it* or *its* to refer to God. These pronouns may avoid saddling God with gender, but they also render God impersonal.

So I am left with using pronouns that are freighted with gender to describe God. Traditionally, God has been described overwhelmingly using masculine imagery and pronouns: God is Father, King, and Lord. Therefore, God is also identified with words like *he* or *his*. Because I love the mystical tradition—the writings and teachings of mystics who lived centuries ago—I tend to overlook the masculine bias in the tradition. I suppose that, because I'm a man, it's easier for me to do so. But I know that, for many people—male as well as female—the use of overwhelmingly masculine language for God is a source of struggle and pain. I believe one of the reasons why William Paul Young's *The*

Shack became a runaway bestseller is because it presented God in a vividly maternal, feminine way. For everyone who has ever had difficulty relating to God the Father (usually because of painful experiences relating to men, or fathers, here on earth) this idea of the motherhood of God is deeply healing.

Ironically, however, as much as some people find this inclusive or feminine language to be healing or comforting, others resist it, usually because it is unfamiliar and therefore seems to be a stumbling block to prayer.

So what to do? I want to include everyone in this conversation about the contemplative call. If I limit myself to just the traditional/ masculine language, I am, in effect, ignoring the pain of those who are alienated by this way of talking about God, as well as ignoring the truth that God transcends human gender—which means that using exclusively masculine words for God is actually a distortion of the fullness of the Divine mystery. Yet, if I decide to use feminine language in place of the masculine language, aren't I just trading one distortion for another? Advocates of feminine language point out that, after thousands of years of male bias within Christianity, perhaps a little bit of distortion in the opposite direction may be acceptable! Whenever I quote from the Bible or the writings of the mystics, however, the male language will crop up again.

Meanwhile, some writers in our day have tried to use creative words like *Mother-Father-God* in an effort to be more inclusive. While I can appreciate their good intentions, I personally find such terminology to be rather clumsy and artless.

Basically, there is no ideal solution to the God-and-gender problem. For the purposes of this book, because so much of the material I am working with comes out of the historical body of Christian mystical literature, I will often be using the old language—masculine warts and all. For my readers who find this language difficult, I humbly beg your forgiveness. For all of us, no matter how traditionalist or progressive we may be in regard to this question of how we speak of God, it is a helpful spiritual exercise to remember that the fullness of the mystery of God can never be adequately contained within the puny confines of human language (including human ways of speaking about gender). For this reason, I try to limit my use of specifically gendered language whenever possible.

If you want some food for thought on this very important issue, I encourage you to consider the writings of Julian of Norwich, a medieval mystic who spoke eloquently about the motherhood of God some six centuries before anyone had ever even heard of feminism or postmodernism. She helps us keep in mind that the gender question is not just something that was cooked up in the last fifty years or so. For a more contemporary exploration of the issues related to this matter, see *What Language Shall I Borrow?* by Brian Wren.

Part One

Recognizing the Call

The Call of the Mysteries

Life is filled with mystery.

Probably the biggest mystery of all is the simple fact that we exist. Why should there be something instead of nothing? Why are there mountains and waterfalls and forests and beaches? Why do the heavens exist, filled with planets and stars and galaxies? The sheer reality of nature, of the cosmos, is basically a mind blower.

If you haven't already had the privilege, someday may you be present at a birth. Even the birth of animals is wondrous. But the birth of a human being? Wow! Sure, we have plenty of science that can help us understand the processes of reproduction, of cell division and growth, of the development of an embryo to a fetus to the world shattering moment when the baby emerges from its mother. But the science just helps us to understand the processes; it cannot explain the mystery—the joy, the wonder, the beauty—of a new life, emerging with eyes dancing full of light and a smile (or a cry) to greet the world. Like nature itself, birth is a profound mystery.

Fast forward to the other end of life. For death, too, is a mystery. There's the obvious enigma that none of us has a very clear sense of what to expect when our time comes. Sages and saints from around the world have offered up various ideas about what happens— from reincarnation to resurrection to never-ending rest. And some researchers have collated stories of unusual occurrences during life-threatening trauma or illness, leading to popular books about near-death experiences—traveling through a tunnel to a Being of Pure Light, and so forth. But all these teachings and speculations cannot erase the profound silence of someone who simply stops breathing. Like birth, death is something that, when encountered, can usher us into a powerful sense of wonder.

Death can be a harrowing, terrifying mystery, for we mourn those we've lost and we fear the loss of others (and of ourselves). Another painful mystery is the mystery of suffering. From the raw jagged edge of grief or a broken heart, to the agony of unrelenting back pain or fibromyalgia, to the slow undoing of dementia or the murky despair that characterizes a deep clinical depression—there seems to be no end to the ways in which suffering can constrict a life or vanquish joy. Even when torment is relieved, it can leave physical or psychological scars. Why do we suffer? Why must those we love feel such pain? What can we do, when it seems that there is nothing that can be done? These questions defy easy answers, if they can be answered at all. And when we resort to the canned comforts of religion ("God has a purpose in this"; "Your faith will see you through"), we run the risk of sounding glib and out of touch. Yet even in its darkest forms, suffering can be a threshold to a most profound place of wonder and awe.

Before the mysteries of death and suffering tempt us into cynicism or despair, consider also one of the most blithesome of mysteries—the mystery of love. That the person who causes my heart to skip a beat can feel the same way about me—words simply cannot describe the joy, the excitement, the reverie, and the hope that love brings into our souls. Love fills a drab world with color and brings a song to the most cacophonous of settings. It is a force for healing by which our hearts are refreshed and renewed. Best of all, love takes many forms, each filled with its own grammar of delight. Beyond the love of sexual and romantic union, there is the love of parents and children, the love of family and friends, of pets, of homeland and nation. We love people, places, and things, and our loves form who we are.

And yet, who can explain love? Why do two people fall in love, while another two simply cannot hit it off? What inspires passion? Or sustains it? Or repairs it when it is wounded? We cannot force ourselves to love any more than we can compel ourselves to be happy, and yet to love is at the heart of being human.

Another mystery that takes many forms is the mystery of creation (creativity). This is related to the foundational mystery of existence, for all things seem to have some sort of beginning. On a strictly human level, however, creation defines who we are as beings engaged with our environment. Obviously, there is artistic creation, from making music to writing to painting to dancing (among many others). But the mystery of creation is not limited to the fine arts. Creation is all about impermanence and change, and each of us changes the world we live in, in small or large ways, pretty much every day we breathe. A businessman creates new opportunities through his deals and sales; a scientist creates out of her research and theories. Even soldiers can have the opportunity to create peace out of the conflict into which they have been sent. While plenty of life's changes are for the worse (leading to suffering), creative changes appear to generate light, life, and joy where nothing of the sort existed before. How? Why? We marvel and we wonder at such a mystery.

Finally, let me touch on the mysteries of right and wrong, and of mercy. A child doesn't have to be very old before he or she can figure out the difference between what is fair and what is unfair. Nobody likes to get the smallest piece of the cake—and everyone, if we admit it, harbors a capacity for sneaking the big piece of the cake when no one else is watching. We recognize basic qualities like fairness, decency, kindness, and honor, but we almost always fall far short of our own standards of what is right or good. Why is this? How do we unravel both the capacity for goodness and the capacity for cheating?

Closely related to the mystery of right and wrong is perhaps the even more puzzling question of mercy. If we think someone gets mercy they do not deserve, we become indignant—but if the tables are turned and *we* are the ones in judgment, we beg for mercy, even knowing how unfair it would be. Mercy is a breach of fairness, and yet it is something we honor and respect, and (when necessary for ourselves) something we desire.

Where, then, do right and wrong come from? Sure, many ethical principles are culturally relative, but others seem knit into the very DNA of humanity. The origin of justice is an enigma, and mercy seems just as inexplicable. Justice and mercy, like each of the other great mysteries of life, bring us to a place where knowledge yields to wonder, in the recognition that these essential components of the human experience can never be fully explained or understood.

All these mysteries shape what it means to be alive, to be human. We cannot explain our very existence, our births or our deaths, our capacities to suffer or love or create, our common recognition of the demands of justice, or the gift of mercy. Yet we cannot imagine life without these realities either. The mysteries of life represent the frontier where the sensibility of our lives shades off into areas we cannot control, cannot comprehend, and cannot manage or contain. Faced with the mysteries of life, we become vulnerable, undefended, open to the marvels that can fill us with the liberating uncertainty of wonder. And even though we live in a world that tries to manage or at least contain the mysteries—hiding birth and death away, medicating the suffering, putting creative folks on pedestals, and settling for a legal system that reduces ethics to a conflict between competing interests—despite all our efforts to control every aspect of our lives, the mysteries are never very far away. They crop up when we least expect them—when we meet someone new and fall in love, when an old friend dies suddenly, when a sudden flash of inspiration leads to the creation of an artistic masterpiece. We never know—literally from one moment to the next—when the mysteries will crack our safely constructed lives wide open. And we never know whether they will fill us with joy or with pain. But they always fill us with wonder.

To mystics, the mysteries of life are our teachers. It's no accident that *mysticism* and *mysteries* are such closely related words, both evolving from the same Greek root. What makes something a mystery is that it is hidden from the peering, penetrating efforts of the human mind to analyze, categorize, and understand everything. Mysteries defy any kind of mental classification. They point to an inscrutable reality that is beyond our mental or physical grasp.

Here's a comment that Saint Bernard of Clairvaux, a monk of the twelfth century and a renowned mystic, once made about nature—one I believe could just as easily be applied to any of life's mysteries. "Believe me as one who has experience," said Bernard, "you will find much more among the woods than ever you will among books. Woods and stones will teach you what you can never hear from any master."[5] Strong words from a man known for his preaching and teaching skills! Consider this: Bernard is not rejecting the kind of wisdom or understanding that can be found in books or from a spiritual director. He just recognizes that nature—even the silence of "woods and stones"—is an even greater teacher. And, of course, it may be the *silence* of the woods that Bernard is praising (in the pages to come, we will look at silence in depth).

But I think it is just as likely that it is the *mystery* of nature that appealed to this medieval mystic. And all the mysteries—not just the beauty of the forest, but also the awe-inspiring realities of birth and death and suffering and love and all the rest—can teach us better than any book or master. For the mysteries open us up; that is to say, they evoke in us a sense of wonder. And wonder is a key to the contemplative call.

Discerning the Caller

E mbodied within the wonder that the mysteries of life evoke in us is the possibility of discerning the source of all the mysteries. For the different mysteries of life open us up to what the Lakota Sioux called *Wakan Tanka*, the Great Mystery. Like Jews and Muslims, Christians recognize the Great Mystery as God.

Right away, we encounter one of the paradoxes of mystical spirituality: God is a mystery, the ultimate mystery, the Great Mystery. Yet God is not an abstract force or idea. We can encounter God in a direct and personal way. God relates to us personally. This is why we can talk about a contemplative call. If God were only a force (like something George Lucas dreamed up), it would make no sense to say, "God is calling." A *call* implies a *caller*. This is an important distinction to bear in mind, for contemplation—at least in its Christian form—concerns something far deeper than just having awesome spiritual experiences. It is a call to intimacy with God. Intimacy with God can mean many things, and that may include some amazing moments of insight, or ecstasy, or Divine union. Or it may not. God is what matters, and any experience of God is secondary.

If we take Ruth Burrows at her word, then we are faced with this idea that *God is longing* to give us the mystical life. But what does that mean? And how can I relate it to my own sense of spirituality?

I took Saint Bernard's idea that the woods and stones are our best teachers and expanded it to include all of life's mysteries for a simple reason. At the beginning, we may not have much of a sense of God in our lives, but chances are that we *have* had a sense of awe, of wonder, of marveling at the mysteries of life. When it comes to embarking on the spiritual journey, start where you are. From there, work backward to see where you've come from, and that may give you insight into where you're going.

As I noted in my Introduction, I assume that, because you are choosing to read this book, you have some sense of this mysterious longing of your own. Perhaps you have enough of a sense of religious vocabulary that you can say: "I long for God." Or perhaps the word *God* scares you a bit, and you feel more comfortable saying, along with C. S. Lewis, that you long for Joy (with a capital J)—a longing that, in itself, is a way of recognizing the elusive presence of this Joy. For that seems to be the key to this mysterious longing—a longing we can't put into words: even the *experience of longing itself* somehow satisfies this desire. The Germans have a word for it: *sehnsucht*, a word that cannot be adequately translated into English but that has a meaning more or less of inconsolable longing. It is a precious longing, however. As C. S. Lewis puts it: "This sweet Desire cuts across our ordinary distinctions between wanting and having. To have it is, by definition, a want: to want it, we find, is to have it."[6]

Now, here is the kicker. The longing we sense for God is a gift given to us by God, out of God's longing for us. God desires us and gives us *sehnsucht* as a way of calling to us. Our yearning for God is a

Answering the Contemplative Call

mirror image of God's yearning for us. But we are the mirror—the yearning starts with God and arises within us as a *response*.

To put it in human terms, the mystical path is the path of love between you and God. But in the great party of life, *God notices you first*. You go about your life, having fun, doing your thing. And God longs for you; God loves you so much. But like any other would-be lover, God sets about trying to get your attention. Of course, being loving and kind, God will never force himself on you or anyone. God wants your *free response* to Divine love. So how does God "flirt" with you? Simply by giving you a taste of God's own longing.

It is my belief that all people have this longing, this *sehnsucht*, encoded within them. Some may go through life ignoring the hunger poised inside their souls. And for a variety of reasons, many others may refuse to interpret it as a longing for God. Some may call it lust for life or the urge to create, or may even misinterpret it as a hunger for sensual pleasure, which, if handled poorly, can lead to addiction rather than to liberation. But some of us are fortunate enough to recognize this delicious longing as an invitation from the Great Mystery, from the One who longs for us with an even greater longing. When we make this recognition, we take the first important step toward discerning—and responding to—the contemplative call.

Saint Teresa of Avila speaks about the soul being a mirror, based on a vision she received:

> Once while I was reciting with all the Sisters the hours of the Divine Office, my soul suddenly became recollected; and it seemed to me to be like a brightly polished mirror, without any part on the back or sides or top or bottom that wasn't totally clear. In its center Christ, our Lord, was shown to me . . . I saw him clearly in every part of my soul, as though in a mirror. And this mirror also—I don't know how to explain it—was completely engraved

upon the Lord Himself by means of a very loving communication I wouldn't know how to describe.[7]

What a fascinating vision. Teresa sees her soul as a mirror, but a mirror also inscribed on Christ, with "loving communication" flowing between them that she can't put into words. Perhaps it was this mutual longing that she saw. She goes on to say that, even if the mirror is clouded or blackened by sin, Christ remains present in her soul. Indeed, even when we cannot discern our own longing, this connection with the Divine mystery remains encoded in our hearts.

So if we are mirrors, our job is to offer as clean and clear a reflection as we possibly can. The light shines on us, and we are meant to offer it back. Part of this task of recognizing the caller is making sure the mirror is clean. The fourteenth-century German mystic John Tauler has some insight for us here:

> If my eye is to receive an image, it must be free from all other images; for if it already has so much as one, it cannot see another, nor can the ear hear a sound if it be occupied with one already. Any power of receiving must first be empty before it can receive anything.[8]

We have to create space within us to receive the caller. Put in spiritual terms, we need to open our hearts to receive the presence of God, shining in us, within us, and through us. We need to be like Mary of Nazareth, opening ourselves up so that our very bodies can offer hospitality to Christ. Like Mary and Martha of Bethany, like Zacchaeus the tax collector, like Simon the leper, we are invited to receive God— within us. This is not a mental game, as if we just have to think, "God is inside me," to make it so. After all, God is everywhere, so God is already inside you (and me, and everyone else) whether we know it or not, whether we like it or not.[9] Therefore the key is to learn how to recognize God's presence and, in recognizing that presence, choose to embrace it, respond to it, and love it. And the only reason to love. God's presence is because we love God.

Like any other mirror, if the surface of our inner looking glass is clean, we are more likely to be able to see what is reflected within it. If we want to recognize the presence of God within us—what the tradition calls the "image and likeness" of God—then we need to make sure to clean our mirrors. Please remember: I am not saying that, if you do a good job cleaning your mirror, God will somehow show up, which otherwise he would not do. Far from it! No, God has already shown up, for God loves you and is longing for you and desires you. Cleaning the mirror doesn't change God in the slightest; it only changes you. Even if you do nothing at all, nothing different, make no effort to wipe the mirror clean, you may still discern God's mysterious presence within you. It's possible, and it has happened before. But if you're already aware of the longing in your heart, then why not do something about it? Make the effort that Tauler recommends: clear the clutter in your ears and mind and heart to create space to hear the contemplative call, whispered to you from deep within you.

I've organized this book in a linear way: first recognize the call; then prepare for the journey; then embark on the adventure. But the mystical life is simply not that tidy and clear-cut. Contemplation is more like a spiral than a line; you keep returning to the places you've been, even as you slowly progress on the journey of your life. And so, when we talk about cleaning the mirror of our souls so that we can recognize God's call, we are talking about some of the same steps that will reappear when we get to the embarking-on-the-journey stage.

How do we clean the mirror, then? Probably the easiest way is to make the effort to love. Love yourself, and love your neighbors as yourself. Reach out especially to those who seem, or feel, unloved. But the three tasks I invited you to do are also helpful: spend some time getting to know silence (compare that to Tauler's idea that, in order to hear something, your ears need to be unoccupied); make an effort to pray; and make an effort to grow (that's a subset of "love yourself"). None of these tasks comes with a guarantee to open your eyes suddenly to God's ongoing presence in your life. But they are all helpful ways of clearing the mirror.

Wake Up

Thomas Merton had this to say about the contemplative call: "We become contemplatives when God discovers Himself in us."[10] In other words, when God's longing for us connects with our longing for God, we enter the mystical life. All that remains is for us to wake up to this fact.

Another twentieth-century mystic, Evelyn Underhill, devoted a chapter of her classic book *Mysticism: A Study in the Nature and Development of Spiritual Consciousness* to this topic. "First in the sequence of the mystic states," she notes, "we must consider that decisive event, the awakening of the transcendental consciousness."[11] This is not a one-size-fits-all process; such an awakening can come gradually or suddenly, peacefully or with much travail, to someone who is already religious in a conventional sense or to someone who has no idea what a pew is. Consider the process of physically waking up from sleep; it doesn't matter if you gradually arouse yourself from a restful slumber, or if you are startled into alertness by the violent, clanging buzz of an alarm clock. You were asleep, and now you are awake. Waking up, whether gently or abruptly, is a classic way of describing the launch of a meaningful, intentional spiritual life.

This is not just a Christian metaphor, either. The word *Buddha* literally means "the awakened one." The enlightenment that came to Siddhartha Gautama as he sat under the Bodhi tree was a truly profound awakening.

So when we talk about your call—your destiny, encoded deep in the hidden recesses of your soul—the first step to finding it is waking up.

When Saint Bernard wrote about the wisdom of the stones and the trees, he was saying that nature can be one of our best sources for contemplative insight. With this in mind, if we want to understand spiritual awakening, perhaps the best way to approach it may be to consider the nature of waking up—that is to say, the ordinary, physical activity of the human body waking up after having been asleep.

What does it mean to awaken? It's about becoming alert, rousing your awareness, paying attention, and noticing what's going on. Although Underhill's language is a bit esoteric, I think she's on the mark. Spiritually speaking, waking up is a metaphor for adopting what she calls a transcendental or heightened level of consciousness. When our bodies are asleep, we enjoy a lower level of consciousness than when we are awake—our brain waves are slower, our perception is dulled, and our mental functions like thought and imagination shut down. Obviously, physical sleeping does not entail the *complete* cessation of consciousness. Dreaming is an important part of sleep, and basic survival functions remain in place so that strange noises, fire, or other disturbances will readily pierce the veil of slumber. The transition from waking to sleeping consciousness (and back again) is not so much an off-on switch as it is a rheostat dial, with consciousness slowing down and speeding back up in relation to the body's state of rest or arousal.

So even in the most down-to-earth, physical sense of the term, awakening entails moving from a lower to a higher level of awareness, alertness, or consciousness. And just as physically waking up is about revving up your mind and body to face a new day, so a spiritual awakening is a process of allowing a higher degree of attention to shape your life. I choose the word *allowing* intentionally, for spiritual awakening is not something we choose to do, like deciding to have lunch at the burrito joint instead of the pasta place. Spiritual awakening, like pretty much every significant aspect of the mystical way, is a gift we receive, not a goal we attain.

It is a necessary gift. Awakening entails more than just recognizing that we yearn for God—or that our longing for God reveals the Divine presence within us. It gives us the clarity we need to pay attention to that elusive and mysterious presence. Such attentiveness means listening to the silence in our hearts and engaging in the process of love—for it is love that unveils that place deep within us where our longing and the Divine longing meet.

Spiritual awakening is not something we can casually summon the way a blind woman calls to her guide dog; but it *is* something we can prepare ourselves to receive. And when I speak about it being a gift, that's not to say that some people get the gift and others don't. "God is longing to give it to *all* of us," Ruth Burrows reminds us. So the interesting question is: what do we do in order to receive this gift?

Underhill wisely points out that spiritual awakening, even if it seems sudden and world shattering, is generally part of a long process. Think of the Buddha. His mind-blowing moment beneath the tree came, not only after weeks of meditation, but also after years of inner restlessness and searching. Great spiritual memoirs—from Saint Augustine's *Confessions* to Thomas Merton's *Seven Storey Mountain* to Anne Lamott's *Traveling Mercies*—are classic, not only because they tell of people who undergo profound shifts in consciousness and awakening, but also because they acknowledge that such aha! moments typically come after long periods of questioning and struggle. Sometimes the most profound events in our spiritual lives come at the *end* of life, as in the case of Thomas Aquinas (more on that in the next chapter). So when we talk about enlightenment, or awakening, or conversion, or *metanoia*, or any of a dozen other terms that can be applied to decisive spiritual transformations, it's important to step back and consider how this is *a process*.

I once saw a greeting card that said on the outside: "Be gentle with yourself." This was followed by this message inside: "Change takes time." The card was marketed as a sympathy card for someone bereaved, but I think its message is rather universal. Do you want to respond to the call hidden deep within you—to embrace the mysteries of God and conduct your life according to the wisdom of the mystics? Then be gentle with yourself. Change takes time.

Because, you see, all the fancy words about what can emerge in the spiritual life—conversion, enlightenment, salvation, transfiguration, mystical union—all boil down to *change*. When you answer the contemplative call, your life changes. This transformation may come gradually, or it may be shattering in its suddenness. And while we may recognize this change as something we initiate ourselves (like making the resolve to stop drinking or to lose weight) because it seems to be an outgrowth of our longing, please try to bear in mind that the impetus for spiritual change actually comes *to* us, initiated by God and hurled into our lives. And perhaps that's the scariest part of all. We mortals love to be in control—which means that, whatever changes shape our lives, we want to be the ones in charge. Change is easy when it's your idea. But when someone else makes the call, then suddenly it doesn't feel quite as safe.

"When we do get there, we almost wonder how we got there," muses the Franciscan author and contemplative Richard Rohr.

> We know we did not *do* anything nearly as much as we know we were *done unto*. We are being utterly and warmly held and falling helplessly into a scary mystery at the very same time—caught

Answering the Contemplative Call

between profound desire and the question, "Where is this going to take me?" It has been said many times that, after transformation, you seldom have the feeling you have found anything. It feels much more like Someone found you![12]

Indeed. We search for the Divine, only to be found by God. This is the heart of the contemplative call.

Traditional religious words like *obedience* and *humility* have fallen out of favor—in large part because we push back against the idea that one person should submit to another. Obviously, this makes sense on a human level; a democratic, liberal society insists on equality and freedom for all people, and rightly so. But when it comes to the relationship between my finite, limited, mortal self and the infinite, limitless, eternal mystery we call God, then perhaps my American allergy to surrendering control may need some recalibration. After all, my control over my life is really just an illusion.

Perhaps, in order to support our spiritual awakening process, we must remember to take a deep breath and step back from our human lust for control. Instead of being the alpha male (or female), we can surrender to God. I realize I'm treading on dangerous turf here, for the language of "submission to God" has been abused by unscrupulous Christians (and politicians) in the past to assert power and domination over others. When I talk about letting go of our need to control in relation to God, however, I don't mean that we should submit arbitrarily to human power structures or surrender our autonomy to others. It's enough of a challenge to open our hearts and minds to the leading of God.

Three Tales of Awakening

Everyone is unique. We all have distinctive personalities, diverse gifts, different values, particular beliefs. Even among people who hold to the same religious or spiritual tradition, almost infinite variety exists—meaning that there are conceivably as many unique ways to be spiritual as there are human beings.

Because of this diversity, the contemplative call—the call to awakening, to inner transformation that opens us to the living mystery of God—will manifest in peoples' lives in an endless number of ways. This can be seen among the great mystics themselves, for, in the two thousand years of Christian history, the men and women who have lived consciously immersed in the love of God have done so in many different ways. Some have been philosophers, others farmers, and others soldiers; many have been priests, monks and nuns, housewives and poets, even politicians. Likewise, the circumstances that shape each individual's journey of love with God—how they come to recognize the call, how they undergo awakening, and how they respond to the promise and invitation of the mystical life—have always been unique and singular.

To begin to appreciate more fully this invitation to spiritual awakening—and how this call can transform our lives—here are three brief stories from the lives of some of the greatest of Western mystics—men and women who, by awakening to the mystery, were forever changed by it. Their lives span several centuries and different lands. As you will see, there is much that is similar in their tales, even while each one is necessarily unique. As each of these mystics awakens to a new spiritual consciousness, each undergoes an unbidden and life-transforming change.

As you read these stories, consider the role that recognition plays in each mystic's awakening. Consider how each of them *sees* something new or unusual that triggers his or her *metanoia*—a new dimension of awareness, a new unfolding of consciousness, a new approach to being in the world.[13] At the same time, notice how the *content* of what they see differs among them.

※

On the sixth of December, in the year 1273, the famed philosopher/theologian Thomas Aquinas, a priest of the Dominican order renowned for his brilliant writing, celebrated the Mass for the feast of Saint Nicholas. As he prepared for worship, Aquinas probably saw this as just another late-autumn day, one more step in the season of Advent, or "waiting" for Christmas, signifying the coming of Christ (commemorating his birth at Bethlehem, but also prophetically anticipating his return at the end of time). This particular day proved to be radically different for the aging priest/philosopher, however. Sometime during that liturgy, something unexpected happened. He received some sort of mystical insight, or perhaps heard the voice of Christ, or entered into an ineffable ecstatic state.

We're not sure exactly what transpired, but after the ceremony was finished, Father Thomas returned to his chamber where his secretary, Father Reginald, awaited him, expecting to continue working on Aquinas's lengthy but unfinished masterwork, the *Summa Theologica*. But the philosopher dismissed Reginald, saying he could not continue with the book, for, after having encountered the mystery, "all that I have written seems like straw to me." Like straw! Remember, this is a man who, even today, is regarded as one of the greatest philosophers of his age—if not of all time. What he dismissed as straw continues to be read by men and women who seek the wisdom of the greatest minds of our culture.

And this proved to be more than just some weird, momentary emotional high that would pass in a day or two. After his December 6 vision, Thomas Aquinas left the *Summa* unfinished, and died only a few months later. One of the greatest intellects of his (or any) age willingly fell silent after that single, life-changing engagement with the ultimate mystery.

✳

Almost exactly a century later, in May 1373 (we're not sure of the exact date),[14] an ordinary but pious Englishwoman from the market town of Norwich fell ill with a fever so serious that her priest was called in to administer Last Rites. She lingered for a few days, hovering between life and death. Then one night, still believing that she lay on her deathbed, she received a series of sixteen vivid "shewings" (showings, or visions) of Christ, Mary, God, heaven, and even the devil. This dramatic event—or series of events—marked the turning point in her illness, and she recuperated.

Later, this anonymous woman took refuge as a solitary living in the Church of Saint Julian, and so today she is known only by the name of her Church—as Julian of Norwich. Not long after receiving her showings, Julian wrote a short book recounting what had happened to her;

she revised this work to create a longer manuscript some twenty years after the event. In our time, more than six centuries after it was written, Julian's book—colorful descriptions of her visions, along with her thoughtful, prayerful reflections on their meaning—has achieved renown as a masterpiece of mystical devotion. Her vivid, earthy, and even radical explorations of Divine love—the love at the heart of Christ and the triune God, and what this love means for us—remain revolutionary in their message, even today. Not only that, but Julian's book will forever be significant as the first book written in the English language by a woman. Unlike Thomas Aquinas, who felt compelled to lay down his pen after his life-changing encounter with the mystery, Julian of Norwich felt called to pick up a pen—and to find her voice.

※

Lest you think mystical encounters happened only in the Middle Ages, let's take a look at a life-transforming epiphany (Divine manifestation) that occurred in the midst of the twentieth century to the best-selling monastic writer Thomas Merton. Merton's epiphany took place right in the heart of downtown Louisville, Kentucky.

On a late winter day in March 1958, the monk had come to the city for a business errand. (Members of his order typically do not leave the monastery unless there is a good reason to do so, like conducting business or going to the hospital.) As he came to a street corner in the middle of the bustling shopping district, Merton suddenly felt overwhelming love for all the people passing by, whom he described as "shining like the sun" in his vision. But this was more than some mere momentary fancy. Merton realized, in that flash of insight, that no matter how important it was for him to be a monk totally devoted to a life of prayer, meditation, and contemplation, he had an even *higher* calling as "a member of the human race."

Merton saw, at the center of every human being,

a point or spark which belongs entirely to God, which is never at our disposal, from which God disposes of our lives. . . [it] is the pure glory of God in us. It is so to speak His name written in us . . . like a pure diamond, blazing with the invisible light of heaven. It is in everybody, and if we could see it we would see these billions of points of light coming together in the face and blaze of a sun that would make all the darkness and cruelty of life vanish completely.[15]

Merton calls the point or spark *le point vierge,* from the work of a French philosopher named Louis Massignon. In his writing, Merton doesn't translate the term, which literally means "the virgin point" or perhaps "the virgin heart." It's *virgin* in the sense of a kind of profound spiritual innocence—what Merton calls "untouched by sin and illusion." This isn't a particularly new idea. Others have spoken of this untouched, virgin point. Mystics before Merton have called it the apex of the soul, the transcendent ground, or the inner light. He realized that, emerging out of the *point vierge,* everyone shines with a spiritual light that, if we could only see it, would even tempt us to fall down and worship one another.

As a result of this shimmering moment of epiphany, the entire focus and direction of Merton's writing changed. Whereas before, almost all of his books had consisted of fairly straightforward, ordinary explorations of Catholic piety, after his epiphany, Merton began to write more about the pressing social and political issues of the day—race relations, economic injustice, the dangers of the arms race. He also became increasingly interested in interfaith dialogue, and began to explore the points of connection between Christian monasticism and the spirituality of Judaism, Islam, and Buddhism.

❧

I've chosen these three particular stories about awakening for two reasons. First, because all three involved writers, so it is easier to compare their different encounters with the mystery simply by considering how their moment of awakening changed each one's relationship with writing (but in strikingly different ways). But please don't get the impression that spiritual awakening is necessarily about writing just because all three of these mystics happen to be authors! It only stands to reason that the mystics from the past whose words we have are, naturally, the ones who bothered to write them down. Thus our knowledge of the great mystics of history is going to be skewed toward writers, the ones who put pen to paper.

It is interesting to compare these three writer-mystics because their rendezvous with mystery impelled them all to change their relationship with their writing—although in distinctive ways. Aquinas, the celebrated philosopher, found that his moment of ecstasy humbled him into silence. Julian, the simple woman, discovered her voice and *began* to write as a consequence of her showings. Merton, perhaps nearly as renowned in his day as Aquinas was seven centuries earlier, found transformation in the wake of his epiphany—he kept on writing just as before, but his words explored new terrain, taking on a new urgency and purpose.

What can we learn from these stories of awakening? To reiterate one obvious point: *a mystical awakening changes things.* It makes a real, observable difference in peoples' lives. Out of the longing for God that mirrors God's longing for us, a single, unexpected moment of insight revolutionized each of these mystics' lives forever. Imagine what kind of difference a spiritual awakening could make in *your* life.

So Many Different
Ways to Do It

I have a confession to make.

When I consider the stories of people like Aquinas, Julian, and Merton, my ego kicks in and I start comparing my own spiritual journey to theirs. There is a small-minded part of me that envies the powerful encounters with God that other people have had. I want similar "mystical experiences" for myself.

I put "mystical experiences" in quotation marks because I think it's wise to consider carefully what this small-minded part of me is really after. Is it looking for God? Probably not. I think the lust for spiritual or mystical experiences is what the Buddhist teacher Chögyam Trungpa Rinpoche called "spiritual materialism." It's a subtle form of idolatry. Saint Francis de Sales put it best when he recognized "a great difference between being occupied with God, who gives us the contentment, and being busied with the contentment which God gives us."[16] Saint John of the Cross, meanwhile, points out that "all heavenly visions, revelations, and feelings . . . are not worth as much as the least act of humility."[17]

Here is yet another mystical paradox. Extraordinary, life-changing encounters with the Divine mystery happen. And yet, they can represent a tremendous distraction for the person who is first tending to the longing within. If the hole in our hearts is shaped like God, nothing else—not even a mystical experience of God—will satisfy us. The contemplative call is a call to intimacy with God, not a call to be entertained by spiritual experiences. This is not to dismiss our longing but rather to be careful to point it in the right direction. To humbly and lovingly long for God and God alone—not even for an "experience" of God—this is the path of awakening.

Evelyn Underhill calls a spiritual awakening "a disturbance of the equilibrium of the self, which results in the shifting of the field of consciousness from lower to higher levels."[18] She goes on to point out that a spiritual awakening involves an "unselfing"—a shift from being focused on or obsessed with our own selves to a new orientation toward God, toward love, toward the mystery. This ties in with the importance of avoiding the trap of spiritual materialism. To the extent that we focus on wanting or having a cool spiritual experience, we actually keep our attention focused on ourselves—what *we* feel, what *we* perceive, what *we* enjoy. Recognizing the contemplative call means taking the spotlight off ourselves and training it on God.

The Cloud of Unknowing, an anonymous fourteenth-century guide to contemplation, acknowledges that spiritual awakening is not always a dramatic, earth-shattering process. "Some walk a simple path, routinely meeting the miraculous in the ordinary."[19] Six centuries later, Zen teacher Charlotte Joko Beck called one of her books *Nothing Special*, and that just about sums up the paradox of contemplative transformation. A spiritual awakening is the most special thing in the world. And it's nothing special at all. It will initiate you into a higher or deeper or more intense world. And nothing will change at all—you'll just wake up and realize you've always been in heaven, even in the midst of your most meaningless suffering, and just have never bothered to notice.

This awakening, this emergence of a new and different world, can happen at any point in our lives and at any time during our spiritual journeys. Sure, we usually associate waking up with the morning, but think about it: just as you can be snoozing at any hour during the day, so can you wake up at any time. Perhaps you sleep in so long that you don't get out of bed until noon or even one p.m. Or maybe you do get up in the morning, but by the afternoon you are tired again and so you take a nice restful nap. What you thought would be a fifteen-minute catnap turns into a luxurious two-hour siesta, and you don't finally open your eyes until it's almost dinner time. See? Waking up (in the physical sense) can happen at any point during the day.

Let's keep this in mind as we consider the spiritual metaphor of awakening. Evelyn Underhill suggests that awakening happens at the beginning of the mystical journey, and perhaps most spiritual teachers who speak of this idea of embracing a new and higher consciousness often suggest, explicitly or implicitly, that this happens at the beginning—in the "morning"—of our contemplative lives. But it simply doesn't need to be that way, and our three mystics reveal this to us. Thomas Aquinas received his mystical awakening literally three months before he died. He was not even fifty years old when he died, but of course he lived in the thirteenth century, when life expectancy was much shorter than it is today. Merton, who, ironically, also died young (in his case, the death was accidental), received his epiphany approximately midway through his journey. In fact, it was right in the middle of his career as a religious writer—his first book was published in 1948; he received his epiphany in 1958; he died in 1968. Only Julian of Norwich, who received her showings when she was thirty and then apparently lived well into her seventies (we don't know her exact dates, so we're not sure), can be said to have had an awakening more or less at the beginning of her mystical path.

If spiritual giants like Aquinas, Julian, and Merton can exhibit such diversity in their spiritual journeys, doesn't this mean that God can transform us at *any* point in our lives?

So what makes an awakening meaningful is not that it happens first on the agenda. Rather, it is simply an opening of our hearts and minds to previously unseen depths of the mystery of God, the mystery of Divine love. So if you're reading this and (like me) you've got silver hair, don't think, "Oops, I missed the train; I'm too late for an awakening." That's silly. The mystery can usher you into a startling new world at any time. Or you may continue to walk the simple path of ordinary contemplation. Let your path be your path, and continually seek God on it.

Here's another important point: Aquinas and Julian and Merton all had years of spiritual longing under their belts before their big moments of transformation came. Merton and Aquinas had both been priests for years. Julian, we know from her writing, had been a pious woman who beseeched God for greater intimacy with him. While all three underwent dramatic waking-up transformations, they had been preparing for those amazing moments for literally years beforehand. They were people of prayer, people of faith, who had been steadily preparing their hearts and their souls for the transforming moments for years—indeed, ever since their youth. They had made themselves tender and receptive, willing and able to yield to the call. Isn't that long preparation before the dramatic moment just as much a part of the waking-up process as the big event itself? Even Evelyn Underhill acknowledges that the big moment of awakening is often preceded by months or years of spiritual ferment.

This leads to another point we need to consider: perhaps, for many people, their spiritual awakening is meant to be gradual, rather than sudden—and for those people, such an unhurried transformation carries its own unique blessings.

Think about the process of physically waking up. Ideally, we wake up slowly, gently, gradually, after a nice long night of restful sleep—but not taking too long, of course, for the beauty of waking up is a prelude to a new and exciting day. We want to wake up refreshed, rested, and alert, ready to embrace all the blessings and possibilities of the day to come. Of course, we live in a structured, industrialized society, so this kind of fully rested, gradual waking-up experience is unfortunately rather rare. Many of us rely on the clanging noise of an alarm clock to wrench us out of our sleep and throw us headlong into the new day. If we are lucky enough or mindful enough to get to bed early the night before, then perhaps we will begin the waking-up process even before the sound of the alarm intrudes upon us. Even if we are already moving out of deep sleep, however, the alarm can still be jarring. Then we scramble to turn it off, or hit the snooze button to bargain with the morning, hoping an extra ten (or twenty!) minutes of rest won't make us late for work. And so it goes.

So what are the similarities and the differences between the gentle, natural, slowly-waking-up-refreshed mornings and the almost violent, here-comes-the-alarm-so-you-better-get-moving type of mornings? The physical act of waking up after sleep, whether the time of rest was long or short, always seems to entail a dance between internal processes and external stimuli. Think about what triggers the process of waking up—a noise, a change in the light, a person calling out to you or shaking you, or even a full bladder or the sense of being hungry. These are the "external" triggers that stimulate the end of sleep. (I put "external" in quotation marks because, obviously, a full bladder or an empty stomach are hardly outside of ourselves; they are, nevertheless, felt as some sort of intrusive event that interrupts the suspension of consciousness that forms the essence of sleep). Let's call these triggers "wake-up calls." It's easy to love a mellow wake-up call (the soft voice of the person you love the most, tenderly asking you to wake up), whereas I suspect everyone struggles against the harsh ones (that blasted alarm clock). But whether gentle or jarring, the call is what sets the waking-up in motion.

It takes more than just a call to wake up, however. For those in a coma, all the light and shouts and clanging alarms in the world won't rouse them. So the second essential element to awakening is our response to the wake-up call. My body, my mind, my entire self has to say yes to the summons. The light shines on me, and I open my eyes. Or the alarm goes off, and I bolt out of bed. My bladder gets full, and I stumble off to find the bathroom. So there are two essential parts of the waking-up process: the call and the response.

Now, here is what I find interesting about the idea of awakening as a spiritual event. I've pointed out several times in the past few paragraphs how we love to wake up from sleep gradually and gently, and how most of us struggle against the intrusion of an alarm clock (especially if we're lacking in sleep, which is more and more the case in our frenzied lives). I find it interesting, therefore, that we want our *spiritual* awakening to be sudden and dramatic, rather than gentle and gradual. We want the cosmic alarm clock to go off. We want the cascade of light and the river of ecstatic love to flow through our hearts and minds, filling us with indescribable bliss and joy, expanding our consciousness to the mind of Christ, so that we see everything with the eyes of the Buddha. Anything less simply will not do. We read the stories of Aquinas's ecstasy, or Julian's showings, or Merton's epiphany, or Teresa of Avila's transverberation,[20] and we want our awakening to be similarly dramatic and mind-blowing.

But don't we have this backward? Perhaps if we listened to the wisdom of our bodies, we would seek serenity rather than drama in our desired spiritual transformation. Why is it, I wonder, that we don't seek a harmonious, serene, luscious spiritual awakening that parallels the joyful process of slowly, gradually waking up on a lovely spring Saturday morning when the light is gentle, the temperature is ideal, and the song of birds outside our windows is all it takes for us to feel the call?

Here's something else to consider, concerning the idea that awakening needs to be dramatic and cosmic in its scope. This idea arises from a hidden assumption that such life-changing transitions occur just once in a lifetime. Isn't it at least possible that a spiritual awakening need not be a one-time-only matter? We have this paradigm of the person who was unenlightened, or lost, or otherwise unawakened. Then—bam!—something happens and his or her life changes forever. Saint Paul sees Christ on the road to Damascus. The Buddha achieves enlightenment sitting under the Bodhi tree. Mohammed takes the miraculous night journey of Isra and Mi'raj, carrying him from earth to heaven. And of course, Aquinas and Julian and Merton have their singular peak moments and their lives are forever changed.

Indeed, awakening can often take this change-everything-forever form. But our bodies don't wake up once and for all, so why should our souls? Our bodies go through a rhythm of wakefulness, fatigue, sleep, dreaming, deep slumber, and awakening again, and the cycle continues over and over. There is nothing wrong—and indeed much that is good—about this rhythmic nature of life. And so it is with our spiritual lives. Sometimes we go one step forward, then one step back, then two steps forward, then one step back. Somehow, the call of a spiritual life made enough of a difference to Merton and Julian and Aquinas long before their big moments. God had already touched them enough for Merton to become a monk, Aquinas a friar, and Julian a pious woman of prayer. I believe that, behind every dramatic spiritual awakening, there is at least one—perhaps many—little awakening that paves the way, just like the message of John the Baptist paved the way for the coming of Christ.

Those of us who recognize the mysterious longing in our souls have probably already had at least one spiritual awakening of some sort at some point in our lives, no matter how small or humble it may have been. In all likelihood, we've had more than one. And if now you have a longing to wake up again, that's part of the nature of things.

The Space Between

S omething internal or external triggers your awakening, and you
wake up.

What happens first, before anything else? Your senses kick
into gear.

You hear the alarm. You see the light (sure, you're rubbing your
eyes, you sleepyhead, but there's no denying that it's a bright new
day). Before long, you will be thinking about all that needs to be done,
whether it's the normal round of brushing your teeth, taking your
shower, and getting dressed; or perhaps tasks more unique to the day
at hand, like, "today I finally need to ask my boss for a raise," or "I can't
put off filing my tax return any longer."

But notice—your brain *isn't* the first responder to the wake-up
call. Maybe it's the second responder, but first comes the pure sensation that arouses. The clang of the alarm. The brilliance of the light.
The roar of the tiger in your nightmare. Something *sensual* wakes you
up, and your first response to waking is to listen, or to behold, or
in some other way to receive the sensual stimulation that pushes you

across the threshold from slumber to wakefulness—never mind how sluggish you may be at first.

And this, I believe, is an important clue to the contemplative call. God calls us to wake up, but it's *not* about immediately thinking all sorts of pious and religious thoughts. (Not that there's anything wrong with pious and religious thoughts—but they are secondary to the pure transformation of spiritual awakening.) This may seem counter to how most people think about God and religion and similar topics, because we have been trained, at least in the Christian world for the last few centuries, to approach God primarily with our minds. Thus we think God is all about thinking. If someone asks you whether you believe in God, they are not wondering if you've ever felt the presence of God, or if you love God, or even if God is important to you. What they really want to know is: "Do you *think* God is real?" They want a report of your thoughts and ideas, your mental processes in relation to the God question.

The Bible bluntly describes faith as "the conviction of things not seen" (Hebrews 11:1), but many people interpret this as "thinking about things you've *never* seen." For so many Christians, it doesn't just stop with thinking God is real. The mark of a true believer is someone who thinks all the "right" thoughts about God—thoughts about God's nature (omnipresent, omniscient, omnipotent), God's identity (three in one, the Holy Trinity), or God's character (God is just, God is loving, God is forgiving, God is compassionate, God is merciful, etc.). And then there are more thoughts to think—thoughts about who Jesus is, and the Holy Spirit, and the nature and destiny of humankind, and so forth.

Please don't get me wrong. I'm not saying that we should avoid thinking about God, or that we shouldn't bother struggling to understand God's nature and character. We have God-given minds, and Christ himself said to love God with "all your mind" (Mark 12:30). I take that to mean that we should indeed strive for the wisest, most knowledgeable, and most well-reasoned understanding of who God is and what it means to be God's beloved.

It's just that thinking is not the whole story.

Here's the analogy in a nutshell: when we physically wake up, our brains, our thinking processes, are not the first thing to get fired up. The process goes like this: I'm asleep; the alarm goes off; it disturbs my slumber; I wake up; the first thing I notice is the infernal racket that the clock is making; and *only then* do I begin actually thinking about my new day. Likewise, in a spiritual awakening, thinking about God or having spiritual thoughts is *not* what comes first.

But what does?

The answer lies in a single word that may seem a little archaic, but that needs to be reinstated in common everyday language, at least among spiritual folks: *beholding.*[21]

Here's the proper sequence: God calls us; we are disturbed (made restless) by the call; we recognize it as longing; we wake up (respond) to the call; *we behold the mystery*; and then—and only then—do we start thinking about it.

Bear with me. I'm asking you to consider something that, in all probability, you've never been encouraged to notice before. I'm asking you to recognize just how God is present and active in your life. This may be the most subtle, the most nuanced, dimension of your spirituality. God is not going to beat you over the head with a giant statue of the Blessed Mother. Far from it. God is far too polite and gentle for such histrionics, in nearly all cases. But the apparent hiddenness of God is not evidence of God's absence. God is present everywhere. So God is present in your life, and my life, and everyone's life. And the point behind embarking on a spiritual journey is to discern, to recognize, that mysterious presence—and then to respond to it.

Don't believe me?

Consider this tantalizing passage from Psalm 139 (verses 7–12):

Where can I go from your spirit?
Or where can I flee from your presence?
If I ascend to heaven, you are there;
    if I make my bed in Sheol, you are there.
If I take the wings of the morning
    and settle at the farthest limits of the sea,
even there your hand shall lead me,
    and your right hand shall hold me fast.
If I say, "Surely the darkness shall cover me,
    and the light around me become night,"
even the darkness is not dark to you;
    the night is as bright as the day,
    for darkness is as light to you.

One of the attributes of God that Christians teach their children to believe (read: think) about God is Divine omnipresence. As the psalmist said, in heaven, in hell, here or far away, even under the cover of darkness, God is present. God is everywhere. So God is present, right here, right now, in these words, and in your eyes reading them or your ears hearing them. You are immersed in Divinity, right here and right now.

Oops, I'm indulging in more thinking here—using language to spin a web of faith as a sort of spiritual consolation prize for those of us who have been programmed to think that God is somewhere "up there" or "elsewhere" and not really present in our lives. That's the con, isn't it? We're taught to think that God is far away, and then we're told that, in order to be good little Christians, we have to think the right thoughts about this far-away God—the right thoughts that we have been told to think by our parents or priests or pastors or Sunday School teachers.

But what if we allow ourselves the freedom to return to that brief moment between waking up and thinking? Even if you haven't had a big grand awakening like Merton or Julian or Aquinas had, at some point—whether it was yesterday or when you were four years old—something shifted within you, and God became more than just an abstract concept to you. You beheld God. Maybe this lasted a split second (that's enough!); or, by grace, maybe it became an ongoing part of your life.

If you are lucky (or should I say, particularly blessed?), that sense of beholding calibrated your spiritual intuition, and you became able to check your inner compass and reconnect with God almost on demand. Or, if you are like many others, after that initial burst of Divine connection, the incessant chatter of your mind kicked in—including incessant chatter about God and spirituality—and, no matter how good and holy and righteous these thoughts may be, they have had the sad effect of making it harder for you to reconnect to that pure place of beholding—the virgin point, the place where the boundaries between heaven and earth simply fall away and all that is left is what Meister Eckhart says, in probably the most eloquent description ever of beholding: "The eye with which I see God is exactly the same eye with which God sees me. My eye and God's eye are one eye, one seeing, one knowledge and one love."[22]

So what is the difference between seeing or looking and beholding? Take the word apart: be holding. To behold is more than a passive act of receiving images of light through your eyeballs. To behold implies a profound *engagement* with that which you see. It implies paying attention and truly being present. It implies not merely seeing, but holding—in your mind, in your heart, in your soul—that which you see. There is a fundamental connection between the seer and the seen. And, as Meister Eckhart's words suggest, that connection is so intimate that the seer and the seen are not two.

We have to be awake in order to behold. But we also have to be silent and present. It's not something that a distracted heart or an anxious mind can easily embrace. As wonderful as it is to ponder and reflect on the blessings God has given us, there is a price to be paid for our mental posturing. It removes us from that place of pure beholding. But we can always return. We are always invited to return to the pristine place of clear beholding, no matter how far we may wander away from it. Indeed, this is the heart of the contemplative call: the possibility to behold, as an ever-present invitation from the Divine mystery. But such beholding is not a task for us to complete; it is a natural state for us to remember.

We'll return to this idea of beholding, for it truly is central to the contemplative life. For now, let's look at a fascinating quotation from one of the earliest Christian mystics, the second-century catechist (religious instructor) Clement of Alexandria, who uses language of initiation to explain his understanding of the contemplative call and our response:

> Truly sacred mysteries! O pure light! In the blaze of the torches I have a vision of heaven and of God. I become holy by initiation. The Lord reveals the mysteries; he marks the worshipper with his seal, gives light to guide his way, and commends him, when he has believed, to his father's care, where he is guarded for ages to come. These are the revels of my mysteries! If you will, be initiated too, and you shall dance with angels around the unbegotten and imperishable and only true God, the Logos of God joining with us in our hymn of praise.[23]

Clement's invitation remains good for us today. We can be initiated as well into the mysteries of God. We can rouse from our slumber and find that sacred, silent space between sleeping and thinking where we can learn to behold the beauty of God. And in doing that, we have, in essence, made the choice to embark on the mystical journey.

Part Two

Preparing for the Journey

The Pathless Path

Ⓘn Part One of this book, we looked at the dynamic of spiritual awakening—of recognizing the contemplative call in the longing of our hearts and seeking the elusive presence of God in the space between our slumber and our thoughts. This awakening/recognition signifies the decision to depart on this adventure of falling ever more deeply in love with the Divine. After all, every journey begins with one moment when we commit to making the trip—whether it's across town, or across the world. Part Two takes us from that moment of decision through all the steps necessary to prepare for our voyage.

The first step is to ask a deceptively simple question: where am I going?

As we have seen, mystical spirituality contains this paradox: the God we seek is already present with us, right here and right now. So in a very real sense, we don't need to go anywhere. As J. Krishnamurti said: "Truth is a pathless land"—a declaration that is often quoted by those who reject religion in favor of a personally designed spirituality. But what few people realize is that Krishnamurti went on to say this:

Truth cannot be brought down, rather the individual must make the effort to ascend to it. You cannot bring the mountain-top to the valley. If you would attain to the mountain-top you must pass through the valley, climb the steeps, unafraid of the dangerous precipices.[24]

So there is the paradox: We do not need to go anywhere to get closer to God, for God is closer to us than we are to ourselves. And yet, just as life is a journey, so too our dance of intimacy with the Divine will take the shape and form of a path, a passage, an adventure.

So, again, the question is: where am I going?

If a journey begins with the decision to make it, naturally the next step of the process is to plan the trip. Whether we spend years organizing the pilgrimage of our lives, or just a few minutes throwing together a few details before leaving on an emergency trip, planning our voyage is a task we cannot avoid. "If you don't know where you're going," the silly but accurate proverb proclaims, "you'll end up somewhere else."

C. S. Lewis addresses this issue in a passage in which he expresses his discomfort with the idea that Christian mysticism is the same as all other types of mysticism.

I do not at all regard mystical experience as an illusion. I think it shows that there is a way to go, before death, out of what may be called "this world"—out of the stage set. Out of this; but into what? . . . The lawfulness, safety, and utility of the mystical voyage depends not at all on its being mystical—that is, on its being a departure—but on the motives, skill, and constancy of the voyager, and on the grace of God. . . . Departures are all alike; it is the landfall that crowns the voyage.[25]

And while this passage is a bit too Platonic for my taste (I don't believe we are called to leave the world, but rather to bring heaven *into* our world), I think Lewis's point bears consideration. If we are going to

Answering the Contemplative Call

launch ourselves into the deep waters of silence, meditation, contemplation, fasting, and intensive prayer, where are we pointing the bow of the ship?

The quick answer, of course, is "toward God." But that immediately requires further explanation—for after all, God is everywhere. If we choose a spiritual path that, for example, involves retreating from life, ignoring the needs of others, and even denying our own basic responsibilities (like caring for our health or our families), then most sensible people would agree that something is out of joint. Granted, my example is a bit obvious, but the fact remains that sometimes, people do unloving or unhealthy things in the name of God. "It is of no use to begin any work unless it be brought to a good end,"[26] says an anonymous fourteenth-century German mystical treatise called the *Theologia Germanica*.

So what is the good end of the contemplative life? Several traditional answers are available for us to consider. In the Beatitudes, Jesus said: "Blessed are the pure in heart, for they will see God" (Matthew 5:8). From this comes the idea of the *Beatific Vision*—the blessed communion with God that most Christians believe will be granted to the saved in eternity, but that mystics have always seen as, potentially at least, beginning here on earth. Incidentally, this vision is not a passive affair, like watching a movie or a television show. Evelyn Underhill points this out: "To be a spectator of Reality is not enough. The awakened subject is not merely to perceive transcendent life, but to participate therein; and for this, a drastic and costly life-changing is required."[27] So the end of contemplation is not merely some sort of heavenly reward, but a transformed life, calibrated to *participate* in the beatific glory of God, beginning here on earth. As one Trappist monk I know has said: "Forget the Beatific Vision, that's too static. I long for the Beatifying Communion." Participation in an ever-increasing love affair with God that begins with enlarging our hearts and wills to become more God-accepting and God-hospitable.

Another Bible verse that has inspired contemplatives through the ages comes from the mythic beginning of the Hebrew scriptures, when God first proposed the creation of humankind: "Then God said, 'Let us make humankind in our image, according to our likeness'" (Genesis 1:26). This dual notion of *image* and *likeness* has inspired much speculation and commentary through the ages. Many Christian thinkers have suggested that the *image* of God refers to the innate way in which humanity reflects Divinity, while the *likeness* is related to behaving in a Godly or loving manner. Because human beings are wounded by sin, so this idea goes, we have lost (or at least covered over) the likeness of God within us. Yet we retain the image of God, since that has to do with our being, and not our behavior. Obviously, part of the task of being human, according to this line of thought, is to do all we can to restore the Divine likeness within us by choosing behavior that is loving, compassionate, and holy.

Without getting too caught up in the intricacies of medieval philosophy, I'll settle for a simple tension within every human being: we are made in the image of God, and yet we are wounded and self-absorbed—qualities that obscure the likeness of God in us. So another focus of the contemplative journey can be to restore the lost or obscured likeness of God by embracing God-infused qualities like love, compassion, humility, serenity, and wisdom.

Finally, we can consider the two great commandments as expressed by Jesus:

> One of the scribes came near and heard them disputing with one another, and seeing that he answered them well, he asked him, "Which commandment is the first of all?" Jesus answered, "The first is, 'Hear, O Israel: the Lord our God, the Lord is one; you shall love the Lord your God with all your heart, and with all your soul, and with all your mind, and with all your strength.' The second is this, 'You shall love your neighbor as yourself.'

There is no other commandment greater than these." Then the scribe said to him, "You are right, Teacher; you have truly said that 'he is one, and besides him there is no other'; and 'to love him with all the heart, and with all the understanding, and with all the strength,' and 'to love one's neighbor as oneself,'—this is much more important than all whole burnt offerings and sacrifices." When Jesus saw that he answered wisely, he said to him, "You are not far from the kingdom of God." (Mark 12:28–34)

Love God; love others; love yourself. There is a lifetime's challenge in six short words—and a worthy vocation for anyone setting out on the mystical path.

These three missions—to seek the Beatific Vision (or Beatifying Communion), to restore the obscured likeness of God within us, and simply to fulfill Christ's commandment to love God, others, and self—are really three dimensions of the same calling. And yes, this *is* the contemplative call, for at the heart of our longing for God (and God's longing for us) is the call to love, the call to let go of all in us that is not love, and the call to participate in the very heart of God's love in an ever-deepening, ever-widening communion. So this is our destination—the direction toward which we must aim our travel plans. It's not a goal, in the sense that God is our only goal. But even that's a silly statement, for in fact *we* are *God's* goal. This is a journey without a goal—a journey through a pathless land—but still we walk the path of love. Ah, the sweet paradoxes of contemplation.

Do Your Research

hen planning a trip, you have many questions to ponder. Once you figure out where you're going, you must next determine how to get there. Do you drive or fly? Is this an overnight excursion or an afternoon jaunt? Is it a one-way trip (moving to a new home) or a round-trip adventure (a vacation in the Riviera)? What kind of terrain will you encounter on your journey, and are there sights worth seeing along the way? Paying attention to all the details helps you to give shape to your proposed outing.

At this point in planning an earthly itinerary, it makes sense to consult a travel agent—or at the least to read a travel guide or two. Obviously, the extent to which you do something like that depends on the scope and nature of your trip. If you're just driving to your hometown to visit your favorite childhood haunts, you already know everything you need to enjoy your outing. But if you are planning your first visit to Bhutan, perhaps relying on someone who knows the land, its people, and their language is necessary—at the very least, it will make your trek that much more enjoyable.

For the contemplative journey, like any other proposed voyage, you can do as much or as little research as you wish ahead of time. For a travel agent, you can consult with or befriend a soul friend or spiritual director to walk with you along your path. We will take a closer look at the role of spiritual guidance in an upcoming chapter; once you are fully engaged in the practice of contemplative spirituality, having such a support person in your life is essential rather than optional. For now, I'll just say that it's never too early to reach out to another person who may have more knowledge or experience about the contemplative life—a priest, a minister, a monk or nun, or even a layperson. Their external roles in the Christian community are not nearly as important as their commitment to the life of prayer and their gift for sharing the life with others. You will likely find such persons in your own neighborhood, even if they do not bother with the trappings of "spiritual direction." If you know of such a prayerful person, consider seeking him or her out for advice and counsel. It can be of tremendous value.

As valuable as having someone to guide you may be, another important resource for an aspiring contemplative is the rich heritage of writings by the great mystics and contemplatives through the ages. The books, poetry, sermons, and other writings of the mystics are truly our "travel guides" as we seek to pursue the mystical path.

Christian mystical literature begins with the Bible. Significant portions of the Bible—including the Psalms, the Song of Songs, the Gospel of John, and the letters to the Ephesians and the Colossians—are notable for their particularly mystical orientation. But even the more prosaic books in the Bible are mystical, in the sense that they represent the sacred writings of our ancestors, whose longing for God has inspired contemplatives of every age since. Many other mystical writings emerged over the centuries that followed—spiritual classics that we can read now, not only to help us in our own spiritual journeys, but also to shed light on the insights and vision of the contemplatives who have gone before us. Here is a very brief list of some of the most remarkable of mystical writings, all generally available in English translation:

- *The Sayings of the Desert Fathers and Mothers.* In the third and fourth centuries, numerous Christians abandoned life in the cities of the Roman Empire to retreat into desert or wilderness settings to devote their lives wholly to prayer and contemplation, often in solitude. These spiritual pioneers, now known as the Desert Fathers and Mothers, left behind a large body of writing, much of which consists of simple stories and parables that point to the spiritual wisdom that was passed down from the elders to their students and followers. One of the greatest of the Desert Fathers, Evagrius Ponticus, wrote clearly about the importance of silence and contemplation in the life of prayer. Another important mystic associated with the desert tradition, John Cassian, taught a method of scripture-based prayer that became the foundation of the contemplative practice now known as centering prayer.[28]

- *The Early Cistercian Fathers.* In 1098, a monastery was founded in Citeaux, France, that became the first of a great order of monks: the Cistercians. In their first century, the Cistercians produced three mystics whose writings remain relevant to us today: Bernard of Clairvaux, who wrote eloquently about the love of God; Aelred of Rievaulx, who recognized that Divine love could also be found in human spiritual friendships; and William of St. Thierry, whose writings on the contemplative life of monks can give insight even to non-monastics today.

- *The English Mystics.* The fourteenth century in England was a particularly fruitful time for spiritual writing. Three mystics in particular deserve our attention: Walter Hilton, an Augustinian

Answering the Contemplative Call

friar whose writings reveal an astute understanding of the psychology of spirituality; Julian of Norwich, the visionary woman whose showings, or revelations, express a lyrical and poetic statement of Divine love; and *The Cloud of Unknowing*, a practical instruction manual on the practice of contemplative prayer by an author who remains anonymous.

- *The Spanish Mystics.* The sixteenth century was a time of crisis in Europe, as the Protestant Reformation led to conflict and bloodshed. In Spain, however, that century produced three of the greatest mystics in the history of Christianity: Ignatius of Loyola, founder of the Jesuits, whose writing explored using Bible-centered visualization as a tool for discernment; Teresa of Avila, a Carmelite nun whose writings on prayer and the mystical life are colorful and accessible; and John of the Cross, another Carmelite whose work explores the intricacies of "the dark night of the soul"—the profound sense of loss and desolation that often occurs in the mature stages of spiritual growth.

Other key mystical classics include the writings of the thirteenth century Dominican friar Meister Eckhart, the fourteenth century Flemish priest Jan Ruusbroec; the anonymous nineteenth century Russian manual of prayer in novel form called *The Way of a Pilgrim*, and numerous writings from twentieth- and twenty-first-century contemplatives like Evelyn Underhill, Thomas Merton, Richard Rohr, and Cynthia Bourgeault.

This list is extremely limited (for a longer list of the great Christian mystics and contemplatives, see the appendix of *The Big Book of Christian Mysticism*) and is offered here only as a brief overview of the riches of contemplative writings found in Christian history. Mystical writers have left us wonderful poetry, insightful biographies, devotional literature, accounts of visions and supernatural events, and instructions for honing your own practice of contemplative prayer.

Books like *The Way of a Pilgrim* or Julian of Norwich's *Revelation of Love* are as easy to read as any enjoyable novel. At other times, mystical writing can be profoundly complex. The writings of mystics like Meister Eckhart, Ramon Panikkar, and Thomas Aquinas are densely philosophical.

Many mystics simply tell their own stories. It is not surprising that mystical literature is filled with classic spiritual autobiographies, like those of Saint Augustine, Teresa of Avila, and Thomas Merton. Some, like Hildegard of Bingen and Mechthild of Magdeburg, filled their writings with colorful and evocative descriptions of their extraordinary visions. Yet others, like John of the Cross and George Herbert, are justly renowned as great poets, having written lyrical and richly textured verses that usher their readers into the mysteries of their intimacy with God. And of course, mystical writing of all kinds is filled with teachings, instructions, insights, advice, exhortations, and occasional over-the-top preachiness, as the great contemplatives sought to share their wisdom in direct and practical ways with their readers and students.

Some mystics moved beyond the confines of the written word to express their spirituality in other creative ways. Hildegard of Bingen was a gifted musician, while William Blake shared his idiosyncratic visions with the world through poetry and colorful engravings. Pierre Teilhard de Chardin's mystical wisdom is linked to the work he did as a scientist, while Dorothee Soelle and Howard Thurman discovered a relationship between mystical wisdom and the struggle for peace and social justice.

Not all mystics are created equal—thank God, for not all people have the same needs or desires or inclinations or abilities. If you love literature, you may prefer Shakespeare, while your best friend would rather read James Joyce. When we explore the wisdom of the mystics, we encounter a similar breadth and variety. We are blessed to receive the wisdom of those who came before us, and yet not every wisdom-keeper from the past will have something necessary or important to say to everyone today (or tomorrow). But some will—so it is up to each of us to take the time to discover the great insights of the past that speak directly to us.

Moreover, just as not all mystics speak to all people, neither are the mystics infallible. Their writings are shaped by their own limitations and eccentricities. Some are dull, overly abstract, excessively penitential, hostile to those who see things differently, and marred by such ongoing problems as sexism, hatred of the body, and irrational fear of the devil. Of course, no one is perfect, so the errors of a mystic do not render his or her other ideas worthless—but we need to use discretion and careful reasoning when we read the writings of the mystics, so that we can embrace their wisdom while gently laying aside teachings that lead nowhere.

Enough important mystical writings are in print today to fill a small library; you can easily spend the rest of your life exploring the wisdom found in these writings. Reading about prayer and contemplation can be a joy—not unlike enjoying a fine collection of music recordings. If you're my age, you may have a bookcase full of CDs; or maybe you just have several gigabytes of MP3s on your hard drive. No matter. Music, like wine, is one of the supreme pleasures of life, capable of ushering the listener into an almost infinite variety of emotional states. Whether it is a carefully performed violin sonata, a stentorian symphony, or an alto saxophone solo filled with rage and longing, great music is both timeless and visceral, evoking the universal palette of human experience, while anchored in the sounds and styles of a particular culture and time.

Now that I have said all this, consider: wouldn't it be a shame if a musician never bothered to learn how to play his or her instrument because he or she spent too much time listening to recordings? As beautiful as recorded music is, it can never equal the joy and power of music performed live. This analogy extends to the contemplative life, where reading about prayer is always a poor substitute for actually praying. "The hound that runs after the hare only because he sees the other hounds running will rest when he is tired, or go home again," notes Walter Hilton. "But if he runs because he's seen the hare, he won't stop, however tired he gets, until he has caught it."[29] When you read what the great mystics have to say about the glories and challenges of the contemplative life, try to remember Hilton's hound. Don't be the one who gets tired easily, rests, and returns home just because you never caught a glimpse of the hare. Enjoy your spiritual reading—and then put the books down and embrace the silence within you.

Provisions for the Journey

The next step in preparing for your adventure is to pack what you need. Naturally, this depends on the type of journey you're taking. For a day trip in the mountains, a bottle of water, your lunch, and a walking stick may be sufficient, but a month overseas will require sufficient luggage (but not too much!), your passport and other necessary documentation, as well as medicine, money, and other necessities.

And even though we speak of the contemplative path as if it were just a nice little walk in a park, a lengthy pilgrimage is a more apt metaphor than a brief stroll. Indeed, part of the nature of contemplative spirituality is that it beckons us, not on a short little vacation, but on a one-way journey to a new place where we hope to live the rest of our days. On such a trip, the decision about what to take and what to leave behind becomes even more crucial.

This metaphor may seem silly in regard to the ascent to the mysteries; after all, on the inward passage, the only provisions we can bring are our intentionality, awareness, silence, humility, and love.

And those, indeed, are precisely what need to be packed for this voyage.

When the great Spanish mystic Teresa of Avila described the soul as an interior castle and likened the contemplative life to exploration of this mansion, she noted that "the door of entry to this castle is prayer and reflection."[30] So prayer is your passport and reflection your visa. These are the two necessities when entering the land of the soul—the interior dwelling place where we hope to find *le point vierge* and the loving mystery called God.

Both prayer and reflection cover a wide range of spiritual practices. Prayer begins with the childlike effort of simple conversation with God as a benevolent father or mother figure: "Please bless mommy and daddy, and help me pass my arithmetic test tomorrow." But prayer is not just for children. It also encompasses the rich tradition of words offered to God through the centuries: the Psalms and other canticles of the Bible, the daily prayers recited by monks and nuns and other people of faith, and an endless collection of private prayers left behind by the saints and mystics of every age. And there's more to prayer than just talking to God. Prayer goes beyond the words of our own hearts or our tradition when we settle into what has traditionally been called "mental prayer"—an unfortunate term because it implies a lot of thinking, whereas the heart of mental prayer is more imaginative—and silent.

Reflection—the other "key to the castle" according to Saint Teresa—recalls the mirror of the soul (where God's longing for us is reflected in our longing for God), as well as our human capacity to ponder and consider such matters of the heart as the meaning of love, the promise of hope, and the gentleness of true peace. Furthermore, reflection entails meditating on the beauty and goodness of God, the spiritual lessons found in the life of Christ or the saints, and even humbly acknowledging all the ways in which we fail to live up to our potential as children of love. In reflection, we receive gifts of wisdom and insight from God (often through the words and deeds of others) and make those gifts our own.

Two other words that I believe can help us to understand and appreciate prayer and reflection better are *love* and *silence*. Prayer is about communication, and communication implies relationship, and the glue that holds relationships together is love. We love God because God first loved us. And a natural and necessary outgrowth of our love for God is appropriate love of self and love for others. So prayer is about nothing if not love. Meanwhile, reflection is about silence. Remember John Tauler's assertion that an eye, to see, must be free of images, and an ear, to hear, must be free of sound? The space we create in order to reflect the things of God in our hearts is a space of silence.

So prayer/love and reflection/silence are the provisions you need to enter into the inner country (what Martin Laird calls "the silent land") of contemplation. But what else do you need to take with you?

Julian of Norwich provides some insight here. Before the illness during which she received her showings, Julian prayed for several blessings from God, including knowledge of Christ's passion, and even a near-death experience so that she could truly appreciate what he went through in his dying. She also prayed for what she called "three wounds":

> By the grace of God and teaching of holy Church, I conceived a
> mighty desire to receive three wounds in my life: that is to say
> the wound of true contrition, the wound of kind compassion,
> and the wound of willful longing to God. And . . . this . . . I asked
> for without condition.[31]

Contrition is not a popular word nowadays, but it is truly central to Christian spirituality. In short, contrition is feeling sorry for your sins. That's part of the challenge of being human. None of us is perfect; we all make mistakes. And we all have to face the horror that some of the things we do, whether by choice or by chance, end up causing harm, even to those we love. Sometimes, that is very immediate: if I smoke cigarettes, I trash my lungs; if I lose my temper and behave abusively toward my wife, she gets hurt. At other times, this connection can be more subtle—as in trying to discern the connection between living an affluent lifestyle in North America and the ongoing reality of poverty in other parts of the world, where workers live on subsistence wages or farmers grow coffee for Americans rather than staple foods for the local population.

There is an appropriate balance to contrition, however. If we go overboard with feeling sorry for our sins, contrition turns into scrupulosity, which is a subtle form of self-rejection. On the other hand, not enough contrition equals refusing to take responsibility for our own messes. So I see Julian's first wound as a desire to find that balance point—a point at which she could feel enough of a pang over her mistakes that she would take responsibility for making amends and moving beyond them, but not so much that the remorse in itself became toxic.

Julian's second wound, compassion, really takes us back to love. For what is compassion but love? The literal meaning of compassion may involve feeling pity or suffering alongside another, but neither of those acts is possible without at least a basic sense of love-your-neighbor. How can I pity someone for whom I have contempt, or suffer alongside someone about whom I am indifferent? Love may be bigger than compassion, but compassion is certainly a type of love.

Julian's third wound, intentional longing for God, takes us back to the very beginning of our quest: recognizing that it is in our longing that we discern God's call.

So in the end, it seems that your best strategy for the mystical journey will be simply to pack light. Yes, that's a pun; for your contrition, your longing, and your love are all ways of relating to the light of God. And I think you can also make the argument that contrition, compassion, and longing for God are all dimensions of the love that lies at the heart of spirituality. Longing for God is an expression of love for God; compassion is an expression of love for neighbor; and contrition, when balanced and healthy, is a dimension of appropriate love of self.

The eighteenth-century French contemplative Jean-Pierre de Caussade understood the centrality of love in his conception of the spiritual path:

> For those who abandon themselves to it, God's love contains every good thing, and if you long for it with all your heart and soul it will be yours. All God asks for is love, and if you search for this kingdom where God alone rules, you can be quite sure you will find it. For if your heart is completely devoted to God, your heart itself is this treasure, this very kingdom which you desire so ardently.[32]

Caussade reminds us that our journey is an *inner* journey—we are seeking not something far away or beyond ourselves, but something found inside our own hearts. Love and silence are the keys to open the hidden places of the heart, and whatever else we need to take with us are simply variations of those two essentials. A proverb from the Focolare movement (an ecumenical Christian movement known for its outreach to persons of other faiths) sums up what is required for the contemplative path—and the value of traveling light: "Take nothing for the journey; all you need do is to love in each present moment."

Protect Yourself

Traveling is dangerous.

When you go to almost any major city, you need to watch out for the pickpockets and muggers. In some parts of the world, you may need specific immunizations to travel safely, and there are places where you'd better boil the water before you drink it. It is a great joy to travel, but common sense and making the effort to understand the risks you may be facing are essential to protecting your health and safety when you are away from home.

There are simple practical steps that all travelers need to take to make sure they are comfortable and secure while on the road. A friend of mine tells the story of spending August in England; he was from Florida and accustomed to blistering heat during the summer months. It was his first trip to northern Europe, and he had no idea what the climate was like. "I never thought I would freeze in the middle of the summer, but what's warm in Britain feels worse than chilly to a Floridian!" he now says with a laugh. So travel protection can be as simple as making sure you pack appropriate clothes for the place you're going.

Perhaps it may seem counterintuitive to you to think about dangers and risks along the path of contemplation. After all, we are seeking the heart of God within the most intimate recesses of our own souls. What could be problematic about that? Our bias is very much toward assuming that, because God is love and love is good, our efforts to seek God within ourselves must be pretty safe. Right?

Ironically, however, from New Testament times on, the contemplatives of the Christian tradition have always included words of caution and warning in their descriptions of the mystical life. The traditional words used to describe the challenges found in contemplation include sin (our own individual imperfections) and the devil (the transpersonal/cosmic sense of resistance to what is good, traditionally understood as the personification of evil). Talk about sin and the devil is likely to make many people uncomfortable, for understandable reasons. Historically speaking, much of the rhetoric in Christianity that concerns sin, evil, or Satan seems to be abusive or distorted; it seems to be more about frightening people into servile obedience than it is about equipping seekers with knowledge that can help them become more fully united with God. A proverbial saying offers these words of caution: "It is better to light a candle than to curse the darkness." So much of the Christian rhetoric about sin, evil, or the devil seems to be little more than curses hurled into the night.

It is not within the scope of this little book to argue about the nature of evil or the likelihood that we may be affected by forces greater than ourselves that appear to throw us off course on our quest for happiness, love, and purpose in life. It is a simple fact of life: people do bad things. We hurt one another; we hurt the environment; and we hurt our own selves. We are abusive, addictive, deceitful, hateful, and self-sabotaging. We lie, cheat, steal, and are capable of violence. And just because we have made a commitment to pursue the love of God within the context of contemplative prayer does not mean that we are suddenly cured of our capacity for harm.

So, just as love is the one thing necessary to take with you on your trip, the main adversary you must protect yourself against is, ironically, your own self. "We have met the enemy, and he is us," proclaimed the classic comic character Pogo. Even if the devil really is out there tempting us, the problem we have to watch out for is our own inclination to give in to the temptation.

What are the dangers that lurk within us? Perhaps no greater threat to your spiritual life can be found than the capacity of your own thoughts to distort your relationship with love. Indeed, one of the Desert Fathers, Evagrius Ponticus, catalogued a series of "deadly thoughts" that can derail the spiritual life. They include wrath, pride, gluttony, greed, vainglory, envy, sloth, and lust. These, in turn, were later codified as the seven deadly sins (vainglory and pride considered as one).

What's important to consider is how each of these deadly thoughts has, in proper measure, a positive role to play in a healthy life. Appropriate self-esteem is a good thing; but pride or an inflated sense of self-importance is not about self-respect but rather self-aggrandizement. Anger can be an important emotion for setting necessary boundaries, but when it gets out of balance, it becomes wrath, which is geared toward destruction and revenge. Eating, desire for a spouse, and rest are all necessary and good parts of life; but when they become unrestrained, they devolve into gluttony, lust, and sloth. Competition between human beings can be a spur to reaching our fullest potential; but when it collapses into envy, it becomes a source of bitterness and jealousy.

What does all this have to do with spirituality? Look carefully at each of the deadly thoughts and you can see how each one represents a distortion or breakdown of love. Either love is missing (as in wrath or envy) or hyperinflated (as in pride or lust); too much love for food, belongings, and rest lead to gluttony, greed, and sloth. The deadly thoughts threaten to knock your entire life off kilter, which includes losing the delight and grace of a loving relationship with God.

So how do you protect yourself from the dangers found in the deadly thoughts? One way is to seek consciously to cultivate creative, loving thoughts that undermine the toxicity of the deadly thoughts. Cultivate compassion instead of anger, humility instead of pride, generosity instead of avarice, self-discipline instead of sloth. Each of us is different, and the deadly thoughts that particularly trouble you are likely different from the ones that pester me. The trick is to cultivate enough self-awareness that you recognize the ways in which you are particularly vulnerable, and focus your efforts on strengthening yourself in those ways. Relying on the support of friends or loved ones can be invaluable in establishing good habits of mental hygiene. It is important for maintaining a sense of perspective to keep in mind that the point here is not to eliminate healthy qualities like self-respect or enjoyment of life's blessings, but rather to prevent or rectify areas where you get out of balance.

Sometimes, it is our spiritual practice itself that can get us into trouble. Some people find that engaging in meditation or contemplation tempts them to see themselves as somehow special or important, particularly blessed by God. Others find that a spiritual practice can be a way of avoiding their normal family, household, and career responsibilities. You don't have to be a rocket scientist to see that these are examples of prideful or slothful thoughts accompanying a spiritual practice—to the detriment of the seeker. Sharing the dynamics of your prayer and meditation with a soul friend or spiritual director can be an important way to uncover—and reprogram—such unhelpful thought patterns.

Making the effort to protect yourself from the distortions of the deadly thoughts is not a one-time task; rather, it is a lifelong habit to cultivate. Such a habit can serve as a sort of homing device to support you as you enter into spiritual disciplines like the daily practice of meditation or contemplation. When an airplane flies to its destination, it never travels in an absolute straight line. Weather conditions and wind patterns can throw a plane slightly off course, and the pilot must continually correct the course in order to reach the destination. These corrections have to be enacted over the entire course of the flight—a two-degree error at the beginning of a flight can mean missing the destination by perhaps hundreds of miles. For contemplatives, paying attention to resisting or letting go of the deadly thoughts is a type of course correction. It helps us reach our goal, which, of course, is the love of God.

C. S. Lewis addresses this concern when he considers how, in his view, different mystics do not always arrive at the same spiritual end:

> Did Plotinus and Lady Julian and St. John of the Cross really find "the same things?" Even admitting some similarity. One thing common to all mysticisms is the temporary shattering of our ordinary spatial and temporal consciousness and of our discursive intellect. The value of this negative experience must depend on the nature of that positive, whatever it is, for which it makes room. [33]

What is the "positive" to which Lewis refers? Finding (or being found by) God, of course. If we allow our journeys to be shaped by pride, or anger, or envy, or sloth, we run the risk of finding only a hollow caricature of a god—an idol of our own making. But if we are robust in our commitment to love, we dispose ourselves to receive the grace of God more fully, leading us to the mystery that we could never find by ourselves.

Find Your Companions

I n the past few chapters, I have made several references to spiritual directors and/or soul friends. Perhaps now is a good time to take a closer look at this unique ministry and how it can play an essential part in your own contemplative journey.

Gerald G. May, a psychiatrist and author of several books on contemplative spirituality, has this to say about the contours of a healthy and full spiritual journey:

> Spiritual pilgrimage involves solitary searching, receiving help and guidance from others, and offering help to others. It is a journey of deepening willingness and clarifying vision. It is a process of reconciling will and spirit. In it, one seeks to find, and realizes with increasing certainty that one has already been found.[34]

The three dimensions that May identifies—solitary searching, receiving guidance, and offering help to others—function almost as an icon of the Holy Trinity. In the traditional way of seeing God as Father, Son, and Holy Spirit, the Father is the lover—the ultimate source and creator, the bestower of love, not only on the entire universe, but also on the other two persons of the Trinity. Jesus—identified as God's Son in the New Testament, where God says "You are my Son, the beloved" (Mark 1:11)—represents the beloved in relationship to God the lover. The Holy Spirit, then, is the spirit of love in fullness, the love proceeding from the Father to the Son (and, as traditionally proclaimed in Western Christianity, also proceeding from the Son to the Father). God as lover, God as beloved, God as love—this is the Holy Trinity. And we embody these dimensions of love when we enter into the solitude of the spiritual life (love), while also seeking and receiving guidance from others (beloved), and then in turn helping others (lover).

Jesus said: "Whenever you pray, go into your room and shut the door and pray to your Father who is in secret; and your Father who sees in secret will reward you" (Matthew 6:6). With this in mind, it is important to honor the centrality of solitude in the spiritual life. We are indeed called to enter into a relationship with God that is intimate, personal, secret, and ineffable—it cannot be put into words. Prayer in solitude and secrecy takes us to the interior desert where, like the Desert Fathers and Mothers and countless monks, nuns, hermits, pilgrims, saints, and mystics before us, we immerse ourselves in our most secret longings, trusting that, there, we will find God who is so secretly longing for us.

But this dimension of solitary spirituality is only one aspect of the mystical life. The other two aspects, receiving guidance and helping others, are as social by nature as the depth of prayer is solitary. These dimensions complement and support one another.

Receiving guidance can occur in formal or informal ways. As we have already seen, one aspect of being guided and nurtured in the contemplative life consists of feasting on the words of contemplatives from the past—the poetry and prose of the great mystical writings. Indeed, part of the beauty of reading the mystics is that it bridges the solitary and social dimensions of contemplation; a book ushers us into the thoughts and values of another, but it gives them to us in our own solitude.

Still, there are limits to what a book can do for you, particularly in regard to the spiritual life. We are all individuals. Thus no book can ever fully address any one person's unique talents, gifts, challenges, and needs. For that matter, a book cannot answer a specific question. While spiritual reading is an important aspect of contemplative practice, it can never replace what Gerald May calls "receiving help and guidance from others."

This does not mean that we have to enroll in seminary, or submit to the authority of a monk or nun or some other spiritual guru. Indeed, the Christian tradition is rather allergic to gurus; almost any spiritual director will tell you that the true director of souls is the Holy Spirit. The job of a talented spiritual director is to create a forum in which the Spirit's guidance can be more easily discerned. The humility found at the heart of Christian wisdom is not just a requirement for those who are first responding to the contemplative call. Those who would guide others are also supposed to be persons of authentic humility. In his *Rule for Monasteries*, Saint Benedict devotes more space to humility than to any other virtue—and makes it clear that humility is meant for every monk, from the abbot down to the newest novice.

Because a spiritual director's job is, basically, to provide humble support for the person being guided so that he or she may more easily encounter the mystery (and guidance) of the Holy Spirit, it follows that almost anyone can perform the role of spiritual guide. Indeed, Kenneth Leech, one of the most respected writers on the ministry of spiritual direction, calls it a "lowly and humble ministry"[35] and insists that the most important criteria for being a spiritual director is not ministerial ordination, or even graduation from a spirituality course, but simply regular participation in the Christian "life of prayer and growth in holiness."[36] This is why one of the loveliest titles for

Christian spiritual direction comes from the Celtic tradition: the *anam chara* or "soul friend."

Guidance in the spiritual life works best in the context of intimate friendship, in which a person whose prayerfulness and holiness you respect is available to answer your questions, offer advice and encouragement, and occasionally challenge you in the areas where you need to grow. So, while such a person may be your local minister or priest, or a monk or nun, you can just as easily find the support and nurture you need from a friend or neighbor at your Church.

Why is this relationship (or relationships, as, especially over time, you may find more than one soul friend who supports you in your contemplative walk) so important? Our society, especially in North America but increasingly in other parts of the world, is characterized by an unquestioning emphasis on individualism—the Lone Ranger ethic. Americans in particular have practically enshrined the idea that "no one tells me what to do" and that the best response to another person giving them orders is to find ways to challenge, ignore, or otherwise flout that person's authority. Ironically, Americans who abandon Christianity for other religions (like Wicca or Buddhism) sometimes—but not always—accept spiritual authority from the leaders of their newly adopted faith.

Christian spirituality is no different from other wisdom traditions, however, in that it sees authority not as a tool for oppressing the young, but rather as a means for passing wisdom from one generation to the next. A spiritual guide, therefore, is a fountain of discernment and insight; the lessons that he or she has learned from years of prayer and meditation can make your practice flow that much more smoothly. A guide can also offer encouragement and support; for spiritual practice, like any other discipline, can at times be dull and boring, especially once the novelty wears off. Finally, a guide provides accountability. If you know that you will be discussing your daily prayer with your soul friend, you will be more likely to stick to your commitment to pray or meditate on a regular basis.

I'll have more to say about spiritual direction in Part Three. But before I finish this chapter, I'll say a brief word on the third element of Gerald May's description of the spiritual life—helping others. For beginners, this probably will not involve offering advice and guidance to others on their prayer life but will rather function in more prosaic ways—volunteering at a soup kitchen or food bank; teaching a Sunday School class; or regularly visiting a nursing home. We can help others in many ways far more practical than just talking to them about prayer and spirituality! Having said that, I have seen even relative beginners in contemplative prayer who are astounded to find others approaching them for advice and insight into the spiritual life. So, once you have started your journey, do not be surprised if other aspiring contemplatives seek you out.

Humility, once again, is the key here. Just because someone asks you a question or two about contemplation does not suddenly elevate you to the status of spiritual master. But it *does* give you an opportunity to help others, just as you yourself have been helped. The longer you walk the mystical path, the more you will be asked to give back to others. There's no need to worry about it now; when the time comes, having your own soul friend will be an important support for you as you are called to be a soul friend to others. For now, just be aware that, eventually, this may well be part of your contemplative journey.

Learn the Language

Perhaps the final task you must complete before beginning a journey involves getting to know at least something about the language, culture, and customs of the place where you are going.

This seems obvious enough when visiting a land where people speak a different tongue. Although Americans have a rather unhappy reputation of expecting everyone around the world to speak English, seasoned travelers recognize that taking the time to learn at least some conversational basics of the language(s) spoken where they will be traveling can make the trip easier and more enjoyable and can open doors to making real friendships abroad. Sometimes, this issue is even important when visiting a place where your own language is spoken.

American English and British English are separated by more than just different accents and, if you aren't savvy about variances in vocabulary, slang, and idioms, you can get into trouble. Consider the word *napkin*. In America, this refers to the square piece of paper used during a meal for personal care—wiping your mouth while eating.

But in other English-speaking countries, this nicety is called a *serviette*. Meanwhile, the common British word for a baby's diaper is *nappy*. So imagine the *faux pas* if you were at a restaurant in London and your toddler dropped her serviette on the floor and loudly announced so that everyone could hear: "I need a new nappy!"

Oops.

And there is more to knowing about your destination than just learning the language. Every culture has its own customs—a cluster of mostly unspoken rules that define polite behavior and govern both formal and casual interactions, whether between strangers or friends. Entire websites exist to point out the kinds of errors that travelers sometimes unwittingly commit, just because they don't know any better. Consider everyday occurrences like getting invited to a party or eating dinner in someone's home. In the United States, if you cannot accept a social invitation, it is proper to offer your regrets politely. People in other countries, however, may consider an outright "no" to be harsh, and may prefer a noncommittal "I'll try to attend," even if it is insincere. As for having dinner in someone's home, if you leave food on your plate in America, it suggests you did not enjoy your meal. Somewhere else, however, a clean plate means you are still hungry.

Even something as simple as body language can be a hindrance to forming relationships. Take eye contact as an example. In America, failing to make eye contact with a person you meet can be interpreted as meaning you are not trustworthy, that you have something to hide. But in other parts of the world—China, for instance—direct eye contact can be interpreted as showing arrogance or lack of respect.

So how do we apply this to the contemplative path? What language do we have to learn? What customs govern the journey into the silence and love of God?

I've given you a clue in the very shape of the questions I've asked. The language of contemplation is the language of silence, and the language of love. Likewise, the etiquette of mystical spirituality begins with the hospitality you show to God, even before you take your first step into the life of prayer.

On the surface, the phrases *language of silence* and *language of love* may seem contradictory. Love implies connection, which in turn implies communication, whether through words, touch, gesture, or actions. Silence, however, seems to be the very opposite of language; it suggests the absence of noise, the privation of words, an emptiness in which true communication or contact may seem impossible.

Perhaps instead of seeing silence and love as opposites, we can take a step back and consider how they may be complementary dimensions of the inner landscape where we hope to encounter God. Like the Taoist *yin* and *yang*, love and silence need each other and combine with one another to form a whole greater than the sum of its parts. That whole is the language of God, which, ultimately, is the language we long to learn.

Perhaps this anecdote from the Desert Fathers can illustrate my point. Once there was a young monk who came to Scetis in the desert of Egypt and asked the holy hermit Abba Moses for a word. Moses answered: "Go, sit in your cell, and your cell will teach you all things." The point, of course, is that the cell represents solitude—and silence. For Abba Moses, silence is not merely the absence of words or sounds; it is the teacher, the initiator into the mysteries of God. How, then, can we learn the language of silence? Simple: by shutting up.

Anyone wishing to walk the mystical path must become a student of silence. This doesn't mean taking a vow of silence. (Even monks don't do that. They may live in silence, but their silence is not under a vow.) Nor does it mean you can never enjoy loud music or a raucous party ever again. Befriending silence is not the same thing as becoming hostile to sound. It merely means opening up a space in your life where all that silence represents—resting, waiting, beholding, not-knowing, and trusting—can be attended to in your own heart, without the distractions that sound and noise (whether external or internal) typically cause.

But silence is not the only language spoken in the land of the Divine mystery. The language of God is also the language of love, of humility, of self-forgetfulness. It is a language in which God is always the subject, never the object. It is a language where every word points away from you and back to your spiritual source.

Hildegard of Bingen, a twelfth-century German mystic and visionary, said: "Many wise men were so filled with miracles that they revealed a great number of secrets, but they fell because in their vanity they ascribed these miracles to themselves."[37] The vanity of which she speaks is precisely the kind of error that ignores the language of love, placing emphasis on the self rather than on God. Hildegard links wisdom with miracles and secrets but insists that such wisdom can be undermined by vanity, because it replaces love of God with an excessive sense of self-importance. So the language of love that is necessary for travel into the mystical places is a language that celebrates God. This can take many forms. It can begin with ordinary religious thinking, encompassing some of the topics that have danced through these pages—compassion, metanoia, holiness, and self-sacrifice. But it is also the language of an important spiritual quality that often does not get a lot of attention in churches—hospitality.

Louis Massignon (the French philosopher who coined the term *le point vierge*) once declared that "the real spirit of mysticism is not achieved . . . save through perfect hospitality." He also linked hospitality with truth, noting that truth "is only found by being hospitable."[38]

In the land where we seek to travel, the language of God is the language of hospitality. It is a language of welcoming, of inviting in, of offering care and nurture to those who come calling. And all this begins with how we choose to welcome God into our lives. Hospitality, like compassion, is a way of expressing love. Any good host or hostess knows that the secret to good hospitality is to put the needs of the guest before your own. This does not have to be an exercise in masochism, but is more of a self-forgetful (read: humble) effort of sharing, of generosity grounded in our abundance. When God comes calling, God is not interested in whatever material prosperity we may or may not have to share. God does not call on us to drink a fine wine, eat filet mignon, or sleep on a feather bed with imported silk sheets. We show hospitality to God by sharing with God our hearts, our thoughts, our values, our relationships, and our dreams. When we give all these things to God, we truly offer God our hospitality. And God takes the things we offer, not removing them from us, but rather transforming them, infusing them with God's own holy presence. And then God gives us back what we have given, only transformed with a new spirit of love and possibility.

Will we make the occasional *faux pas* when we travel to the new land of contemplation? Of course. But, just as a business traveler to China or India trusts in the good will of his or her hosts to overlook the occasional social blunder, so too the love of God will overcome all the ways we fail to learn from silence, to live in love, and to practice hospitality with our very lives.

In saying this, however, I am not suggesting that we are let off the hook. It is still up to us to make the effort to learn the ways of heaven—for, you see, heaven is this land where the language and customs are so different from our own, this land we seek to visit, even though we travel there by following only the path within our hearts. Heaven is heaven because it is where God lives. And this is where the mystical path promises to take us.

So. You have considered where you wish to go, who will guide you on your way, what provisions and safeguards you need, and what you need to learn about the language and customs of your destination. It is now time to set out on your adventure.

Answering the Contemplative Call

Part Three

Embarking on the Adventure

The Mystical Path Begins
with Christ

The first step on the journey into Christian contemplation involves opening your heart to Christ.

In saying this, I am not trying to foist on you a message like "accept Jesus as your personal savior or else you're going to hell." So many people, both inside and outside of the Church, are understandably wary of this message because of its underlying hostility and thinly veiled subtext that Christianity is a system of social and psychological control. But that is not what the traditional message of the mystics has been. Jesus has been loved and accepted by the mystics, not as a way of appeasing an angry God, but as a joyful entry into the mysteries of love.

So why am I not just saying, "open your heart to the mysteries of love" if that's what I mean? I think it's important to keep the focus on Jesus for two reasons. First, it anchors us squarely in the Christian tradition—which is not meant to be exclusive or hostile to other wisdom paths, but simply grounded in what is unique and beautiful about this particular expression of spirituality. In affirming the centrality of

Christ in Christian contemplation, I am not denouncing other paths of mystical wisdom, nor am I rejecting interfaith and interspiritual expressions of mysticism. I myself am very active in the interfaith/interspiritual community where I live. But I think it is essential that we establish our basic spiritual identity as a prerequisite for any trans-religious exploration; for Christians, this means engaging with the tradition of devotion to Jesus. Look at it this way: If you want to be a musician who plays many instruments, that's wonderful. But if you do not focus on one instrument first and master it, you run the risk of being a musical dilettante, playing many instruments, but none of them very well. On the other hand, once you master the guitar, picking up the flute or the piano is that much easier because you have already made the effort to play one instrument well.

Interspiritual mysticism works the same way. If you want to explore not only the wisdom of Jesus but also the wisdom of Buddha or the Sufis or Kabbalah, I am confident that you have a wonderful adventure ahead of you. But begin at the beginning. And for seekers of the Christian mysteries, that means an initial commitment to be grounded in the mysteries of Christ.

The second reason for emphasizing Christ rather than generic love is that Christian spirituality is incarnational—in other words, it emphasizes the essential goodness of our humanity, our embodied status as creatures of flesh and blood. If we focus our mystical longing exclusively on abstractions like "love" or "peace" or "joy," we run a risk of reducing our spirituality to a mental exercise—a head trip in which thinking the right thoughts becomes a substitute for actually living embodied in love.

In other words, the power of Christ resides in his humanity. He is a person to love and by whom we are loved. He is not an abstraction, or a philosophical principle, or a disembodied emotion. He is real; he has a personality, a face, and a heart. Yes, Jesus in the flesh walked the earth two millennia ago, so we relate to him through our thoughts and imagination—but for Christians, it makes a difference that our thoughts and imagination remain oriented toward a real, flesh-and-blood human being (whom we also celebrate as an incarnation of the Divine).

At one point in the Roman Catholic Mass, the priest or deacon says these words quietly over the Communion chalice: "By the mystery of this water and wine, may we come to share in the Divinity of Christ who humbled himself to share in our humanity." Thus, for Christians, the fact that Christ shared in our humanity is seen as foundational to our sharing in the mystery of Christ's—and, therefore, the triune God's—Divinity.

Teresa of Avila understood the importance of basing spirituality on a relationship with Christ. "How much more is it necessary not to withdraw through one's own efforts from all our good and help, which is the most sacred humanity of our Lord Jesus Christ," she stated in her masterpiece, *The Interior Castle*. "The Lord Himself says that He is the way; the Lord says also that He is the light . . ."[39] Teresa understood that, for anyone drawn to contemplation—to prayer immersed in silence, to the yearning for God that takes us to a place beyond language—there is a temptation to ignore the sacred humanity of Christ. We can say to ourselves: "The key to spirituality is contemplation, and that does not require engagement with the Gospel, or the Church, or the Sacraments." And then off we go on our precious, personal quest for God. And we'll have things about half right.

You see, the problem with not focusing on Christ is that, if we ignore Christ, we can also ignore his teachings. And that means we ignore some of the most powerful elements of the Christian spiritual tradition. *Love your enemies. Be not afraid. Do not judge. Abide in my love. Whatever you do to the least of these, you do to me. Truth will set you free. It's easier for a camel to slip through the eye of a needle than for a wealthy person to enter the kingdom of heaven. Whoever would be first must become the servant of all.*

We can also ignore the stories he told (and that were told about him), which sometimes include truly revolutionary understandings of politics and economics. The poor widow who gives away a penny is more generous than the wealthy person who gives a slice of his disposable income. The rich man who dies and suffers torment, only to find the homeless person he ignored for many years resting in paradise. The son who squanders his inheritance only to find his father totally forgiving, even though his brother remains angry and judgmental. The woman obsessing over housework (and angry at her sister for not helping out) who is gently chided for not relaxing and enjoying the company of her guests. And so many other stories as well.

If you grew up in a Church-going family, or have been attending a Church for more than a year or so, these stories and sayings will seem so familiar that you will be tempted just to gloss over them. But the contemplative path invites you to reencounter Jesus with fresh eyes— to see him, not as some magical god figure but as a fully enfleshed, embodied spiritual teacher who, if you truly listen to his words with an open mind and an open heart, had some pretty radical things to say.

The Christian path invites you to embed your spiritual practice— your search for the mystery of God, the longing of the Divine, the mystery beyond the farthest reaches of the universe and within the hidden recesses of your heart, but grounded in the person of Jesus—in his teachings and his values, and in the stories that define him as one with God the Father (John 10:30), fully human (I Timothy 2:5), and fully Divine (Philippians 2:6). Jesus died and, on the third day, rose again, as recounted in each of the Gospels. Then, as recounted in the Acts of the Apostles, he ascended into heaven.

Contemplative spirituality engages with the story of Christ—from the most revolutionary teachings to the most miraculous supernatural events—because, in Christ, we find two powerful dimensions of spirituality: insight into the nature of our own souls, and insight into what is truly possible for humanity if we all could truly love one another the way Christ called us to do. Granted, contemplative practice focuses particularly on the inner work of spirituality, but it is important to remember that Christianity, in its fullness, addresses both the interior/contemplative *and* the exterior/social dimensions of spirituality. Christ taught his followers to find him in the eyes and hearts of the poor, the downtrodden, the hungry and homeless. But he also taught them to recognize that he would abide in them—which is to say, in each person's heart.

For the spiritual life to reach its full potential, the interior/mystical dimension needs to be balanced by the external/social dimension. This is why the Franciscan teacher and activist Richard Rohr set up an institute called the Center for Action and Contemplation, recognizing that spirituality must include both the interior and external dimensions. Indeed, I've seen Fr. Richard more than once tell an audience that the most important word in the name of his center is *and*—because it emphasizes the balanced necessity of both the meditative and social dimensions of spirituality.

It is not within the scope of this book to explore the social dimensions of a relationship with Christ. To read more on this important subject, consult Albert Nolan's *Jesus Before Christianity*, Ched Myers' *Binding the Strong Man*, John Howard Yoder's *The Politics of Jesus,* Brian McLaren's *Everything Must Change*, and Kenneth Leech's *The Eye of the Storm*. The social/external/activist dimension of Christian spirituality is essential, and I believe a truly contemplative spirituality needs an activist dimension (just as a peace-and-justice-oriented spirituality requires a contemplative dimension). In this book, I am focused on the steps you can take to answer the contemplative call, looking for a relationship with Christ found within. It's important to remember, however, that this is only part of the Christian story, and that we need to keep a balanced perspective.

As we look for Christ within, we discover an invitation to move farther on the mystical path. As the twentieth century English mystic Caryll Houselander wrote:

> Because He is in the little house of our being, we will learn
> to control our minds, to gather our thoughts to silence, and to
> crown them with peace, just as we learn to control our voices
> and to move softly when a child is asleep in the house of
> brick and mortar.[40]

And Saint Augustine reminds us that looking for Christ outside of ourselves is pointless if we do not learn to find him within:

> O noble soul, O noble creature of God, why go outside yourself
> in search of Him who is always and most certainly within you,
> through whom you are made a partaker of the divine nature?[41]

The Mystical Path Ends
in Mystery

Two of the most beautiful writings in the mystical tradition are Julian of Norwich's *Revelation of Love* and the anonymously written manual of contemplative prayer, *The Cloud of Unknowing*. Both were written in Middle English (similar to the language of *The Canterbury Tales*), and were composed in the last quarter of the fourteenth century. Today, both books have been translated into modern English and are popular among students of Christian contemplation and mystical spirituality.

Despite their many similarities, however, the two books are remarkably different. Julian's writing is filled with visionary language. It is sensual, grounded in nature imagery (like hazelnuts and herrings, the ocean and the desert), and filled with insights into the nature and ministry of Jesus. She is a sterling example of a Christo-centric—that is to say, Christ-centered—mystic. Many of her visions include her engaging in conversation with Christ or reflecting on the meaning of Christ's actions—as described in both her own visions and in the Gospel story. Julian's spirituality is *kataphatic,* coming from a Greek word that means "to affirm"—which is to say that it is a spirituality based on positive affirmations about God: God is love; God is courteous; God is just; God is compassionate. Even if we are speaking about Christ rather than God, but using positive statements, it's still kataphatic. When I speak about God longing for you, I am making an affirmative statement. Any attempt to visualize God or Christ is an exercise in kataphatic spirituality—a spirituality that is positive, sensual, and based on concepts, images, or statements that we have about who God is and how we relate to God.

You don't have to spend too much time exploring spirituality, however, before you begin to bump into the limitations of the kataphatic approach to God. Paradox and mystery can both subtly undermine this positivist approach to spirituality. Say "God is Father"— a traditional affirmation of Biblical faith—and immediately you bump into a host of questions. Is God not also our mother? Does God have a gender? If not, then isn't this language about God a limiting distortion? It seems that anything positive we say about God probably has lurking within it a paradox or seeming contradiction that is not so much an indictment of God as it is a reflection of the limitations of human language and thought.

Another way to approach God is called *apophatic*, from a Greek word meaning "to deny"—not denial in the sense of rejection or opposition, but simply in the sense of denying that any positive statement about God can ever contain the fullness of the mystery. Apophatic statements are thus typically negative in their formulation: God is not vindictive; God is not limited; God is not petty; God is not prejudiced. Apophatic spirituality seeks to find God without visualization or conceptualization—as if thinking the right thoughts can somehow bring us closer to God. Rather it seeks to clear away all images, concepts, and thoughts about God, rejecting them all as limited and incomplete, and therefore inadequate to help us become truly intimate with the Divine mystery.

As kataphatic as Julian's spirituality is, so is *The Cloud of Unknowing* a masterpiece of the apophatic way. Its anonymous author counsels his readers to put all their thoughts and images about God beneath a "cloud of forgetting" so that they may approach the ineffable mysteries of the Holy One, who nevertheless always remains shrouded behind the mysterious cloud of unknowing. How do we penetrate that cloud so that we can connect with God? By our thoughts and concepts, it is impossible. But by the "dart of longing love," we can reach into the cloud and connect with the source of love. Love takes us to a place that images, thoughts, and concepts can never reach.

Again and again throughout history, mystics have pointed out the importance of the apophatic way—that God ultimately cannot be known in any kind of theoretical or conceptual sense. In the fourth century, Gregory of Nyssa (not only a great mystic, but also a theologian and a bishop of the Church) said: "Every concept formed by our understanding which attempts to attain and to hem in the divine nature serves only to make an idol of God, not to make God known."[42] Nine centuries later, Thomas Aquinas came to much the same conclusion: "Concerning God, one cannot say what God is, but only what God is not."[43] John of the Cross, writing in the sixteenth century, agreed:

> One of the greatest favors bestowed on the soul transiently in this life is to enable it to see so distinctly and feel so profoundly that it cannot comprehend God at all. . . . They who know God most perfectly perceive that God is infinitely incomprehensible.

John was one of the greatest of apophatic mystics, and he cannot resist taking a dig at those whose spirituality is more kataphatic in nature: "Those who have less clear vision do not perceive so clearly how greatly God transcends their vision."[44]

Chief among the reasons we cannot know God is that God is not an object to be known. Kenneth Leech points out that this explosive idea goes back to the Church Fathers, at least as far back as the eighth century: "According to St John of Damascus, God does not exist in the sense that we normally use that word: the whole concept is inapplicable to God since only objects exist and God is not an object. God is known through unknowing, through agnosia."[45]

So which is better? Julian's richly conceptual meditations on God, including the humanity of Christ (which Teresa of Avila reminds us is essential for a balanced Christian life)? Or the unfathomable mystery of the hidden God lost in the cloud of unknowing, whom we can reach by the naked intent of our longing, but never fully grasp by the clever wordplay of our thinking egos?

Of course, it's not either/or. Both the kataphatic and the apophatic approaches to spirituality have their place. In my life, I have known people who are naturally kataphatic in their spirituality, and others who are more naturally apophatic. Sometimes the ones who are naturally gifted at one way of approaching spirituality attack or reject the other way as inferior or insufficient. But that makes about as much sense as left-handed people saying righties are no good (and vice versa). Everyone who engages in the serious pursuit of contemplative spirituality discovers that either the sensual imagery of kataphatic prayer or the vast emptiness of apophatic prayer is the more "natural" way of praying for them. And that's fine. But each of us needs at least to be familiar with both approaches to spirituality.

For kataphatic Christians, the natural disciplines of spirituality include reading the Bible and praying with words—whether reciting established prayers like the Daily Office, or making up their own prayers in a kind of spontaneous conversation with God. The apophatics, however, are drawn more toward the pure sense of silent awareness, which seeks both exterior silence (a quiet place) and the even more elusive interior silence of the heart. Apophatic Christians find silent contemplation to be as spiritually nourishing as praying the Psalms is to kataphatic believers.

Some aspiring contemplatives may discover that their spirituality begins with kataphatic practices (which are, after all, the practices of most ordinary religious observances) only to move deeper into apophatic silence as their hearts lead them away from words and into silence before the Divine mystery. Indeed, this is why I've suggested, beginning in the last chapter, that Christian spirituality begins with Christ—with the kataphatic appreciation of Christ's humanity—but ultimately ends in the ineffable mystery of God. Meditating on the humanity of Christ, and on his teachings and actions, is a foundation from which the wordless spirituality of contemplative silence may most fruitfully grow.

If you are more naturally drawn to the wordless and imageless silence of the apophatic way, please resist any idea that apophatic contemplation is a higher form of spirituality. Likewise, if you take great joy in a vivid, deeply imaginative approach to prayer, don't assume that kataphatic spirituality is somehow the better path. Acknowledge which path speaks to you, but try to appreciate the presence of God in both richly vivid imagery and in the dark silence of unknowing.

All who are in touch with the spiritual longing in our hearts can probably recognize that either the kataphatic or apophatic approach to spirituality is particularly helpful to us. Either we have found normal religious activities like prayer, public worship, and Bible study to be particularly nourishing to us, or else we have found ourselves drawn to solitude and silence, to the serenity of an empty cathedral or a remote monastery where, bereft of noise and sound, we can more readily attend to the mysterious place in our hearts that we intuitively recognize surpasses all normal human thought. Meanwhile, I imagine some contemplatives may be spiritually ambidextrous, finding joy and insight equally in both the kataphatic and apophatic forms of spiritual practice.

You will see in the chapters to come that I encourage you to explore both of these dimensions of contemplation. Try to embrace both forms. Having a soul friend can be an important step in sorting through your own unique calling as a contemplative—whether you feel more drawn to the sensuality of kataphatic ways of connecting with God, or the austerity of your inner apophatic silence. Do not try to force your spiritual style. If you feel more naturally nourished by positive ways of relating to God, accept this and pursue this spirituality. Or vice versa. You may find, in the future, that your spiritual appetite changes; but let the future care for itself. Your task is to be faithful here and now.

However, even if you have a clear sense that your contemplative practice should be filled with (or devoid of) concepts and imagery, give yourself permission to explore all the varieties of spirituality discussed in this book, as well as in other books you read. In other words, read both Julian of Norwich and *The Cloud of Unknowing*. Chances are that you will like one more than the other. But don't give up on the one with which you do not immediately bond. Sometimes the treasures of contemplation are given to us slowly, over time. Do not short-circuit your relationship with God by deciding that you know best how to manage your spirituality. Remember, your spirituality was God's spirituality first.

Befriend Silence

Whether your natural spiritual style is kataphatic or apophatic, perhaps the single most important step you will take on your spiritual journey involves cultivating a home for silence in your heart.

I have met more than a few spiritual seekers over the years who have tried to foster a practice of meditation or contemplative prayer, only to give it up because they find the inner noise simply too much to bear. The truth is, it *is* too much to bear; but the difference between those who abandon contemplation and those who stick with it is often little more than a willingness to keep searching for the silence in the midst of the inner noise. Even after months or years or decades of practice, veteran contemplatives are often humbled by the degree of inner noise—of mental static and emotional turmoil—that persists within their hearts and minds. It seems that the noisy world out there is simply a mirror of the noisy cosmos in here. We've filled the silence of our lives with machines that clatter and media that blares because we all preside over an inner-verse where the cacophony is incessant.

Or maybe it's the other way around. Who knows? The point is simple: our environment is noisy, and our psyches, our souls, are noisy as well. And somewhere in the midst of the din arises the contemplative call. But how can we hear it—even if we are paying attention? Our only hope is to foster silence as best we can, messy and imperfect though it may be.

This is not just a modern problem brought about by computers and jet engines and other noisemakers that have become ubiquitous in our society. Walter Hilton points out that inner noise, at least, has been around for a very long time. "Truly, there is so great a din in your heart, and so much loud shouting from your empty thoughts and fleshly desires that you can neither see nor hear Him," he wrote—back in the fourteenth century! But his recommended cure for inner noise remains worthy of consideration, even today: "Therefore, silence this restless din, and break your love of sin and vanity. Bring into your heart a love of virtues and complete charity, and then you shall hear your Lord speak to you."[46]

I'm not sure that matters are quite as simplistic as Hilton seems to depict them—with sin as the cause of our inner racket, and virtue the key to silencing it. But I do think that "complete charity"—in other words, love—is an important quality to cultivate as part of our quest for the serenity of interior silence.

The good news is that, despite the incessant chattering of what Buddhists call "the monkey mind" (that inner voice that *never* seems to shut up), glimpses of silence can come to us within and in between the ongoing internal commentary. Even if only for a few seconds here and there, it is possible to take a deep breath, relax, be fully present to the silence that lies beneath our mental clutter, and *just be*. Indeed, one of the key purposes behind silent contemplative disciplines like centering prayer is to foster the ability to catch glimpses of the silence—silence that is always present beneath the noise within us. With time and by the grace of God, we learn to rest in the silence for longer moments.

Answering the Contemplative Call

Silence is beautiful. And contemplative silence—the silence to which we lovingly attend in the name of the sacred mystery we call God—is the most beautiful silence of all.

Of course, using words to describe the beauty of contemplative silence is a little like using an electric guitar amped up with plenty of feedback and distortion to interpret a violin sonata. Indeed, by their very nature, words—even when merely printed on a page—function as a sort of anti-silence. Even soundless words on a page can contribute to the inner noise that masks contemplative silence. So my purpose in writing this section is, in fact, to sabotage my own work—to compose words that undermine themselves by encouraging you to turn away from them toward the splendor of the silence that lies hidden beneath them.

When people who have habitually smoked tobacco find the grace to let go of their addiction, they often report an unexpected blessing—a newly revived sense of taste and smell. Without them even realizing it, the taste and smell of tobacco had functioned as a veil, blocking their ability to engage fully with the sensual wonders of their environment. When they finally purge their bodies of the smoke-related toxins, it seems to open up an entirely new world of olfactory and gustatory wonders. But, in truth, these wonders were part of their environment all along. It's not as if, once they quit smoking, God suddenly decided to unfold a more nuanced universe in terms of aroma and flavor. No. The smoke was a mask, a curtain, a barrier that diminished their lives even as they labored under the conviction that they needed and wanted it.

The noise, environmental and internal, that characterizes the world in which so many of us live is very much like the cigarette smoke that diminishes the pleasure of habitual smokers. Although I may write as eloquently as I possibly can about the nuance, the personality, the *presence* of contemplative silence, for those who have not yet touched that silence because of the noise in their lives, my words may very well be just more clamor added to the din. Humbled by this thought, I shall nevertheless offer a few brief words in the hope that they may help you to recognize what lies beyond all words.

In seeking to befriend silence, let your silence be imperfect. Recognize that the silence you find will always be broken by sound of some form or another. I don't believe it is possible for us to find absolute silence, anyway. Find refuge from the din of technology and you will still face the distraction of buzzing insects, barking dogs, or a snoring roommate. Perhaps if you manage somehow to get far away from the organic sounds of living creatures—say, deep within intergalactic space—you may find a place utterly devoid of sound, a place with absolute zero decibels. But what would it take to get there? Some sort of rocket ship, of course. And, even if we really could get out there, all we would be doing is polluting the absolute silence with the roar and whoosh of our technology.

And even if you somehow can find a place with no external sound—in the desert, perhaps, far from any living thing—you will still discern the beating of your heart, the soft rasp of your breathing, the alchemy of your digestive system with your growling stomach and gurgling intestines—and, of course, that never-ending symphony of thought and impressions generated within the theater of your mind. The quieter your surroundings, the more stentorian your inner sounds become. Any sound can become noise if it is intrusive and distracting enough; noise tends to be relative according to the environment in which it exists. In a shopping mall, it would take a siren to get most people's attention. In a monastery, even a whisper is disruptive.

So contemplative silence isn't pure silence at all—no more so than a flat surface is absolutely flat. When viewed under a microscope, even the surface of the proverbial flat pancake turns out to be broken by an endless succession of hills and valleys; it's just that they are so small that they escape detection by the naked eye or hand.

I see beauty in silence because silence is modest—it never forces itself on anyone, it's not intrusive or disruptive. Rather, it waits in the background, behind all noises, whispers, or sounds, whether harmonious or cacophonous. Within the endless possible sounds we can hear, the beauty of silence lies in its subtlety, its ability to reveal its undemanding wonders without aggression or hostility to the one who listens.

This genteel quality of silence makes a difference, especially when we begin a discipline of meditation or contemplative prayer. As I mentioned earlier, a common trap for beginners is to become discouraged by the incessant chatter of the monkey mind. "I can't meditate" is often code for "I'm embarrassed at how noisy I am on the inside, and I have no idea how to get it to stop." Well, here's the good news: you won't get it to stop, so let go of any fruitless efforts in that direction.

What you *can* do, however, is breathe just a little bit of space in between the clamor and din of your thoughts and feelings and inner soundtrack. Don't bother trying to shut up your inner voice, but do insist that it slow down a little—or a lot. What is fascinating is how, as you become more familiar with the contours of silence that lie beneath and beyond the monkey's chatter, eventually even the thoughts and feelings themselves become somewhat translucent, allowing the silence to shine through like light through a stained-glass window. A stained-glass window masks us from the luminous brilliance of the sun, but, in doing so, it gives us a pleasure of its own, a feast of color and image that the light brings to life. Moreover, silence and our interior monologue can sometimes have a similar symbiotic effect; the words we generate inside ourselves can expand into a spacious presence, a kind of luminous kaleidoscope of self-knowledge. Even when our thoughts are troubled or troubling, we can learn to see them against the backdrop of the little silence within us that, through the portal of *le point vierge*, opens out into the vast limitless silence of the mystery we call God.

Contemplative silence is beautiful, not because it lacks noise, but because it gives us the space to find wonder even in the most gentle, nuanced sounds we encounter. When my wife and I sit for our morning time of shared silent prayer, we often hear birds singing in our back yard, or the loud purring (and sometimes even snoring!) of one of our cats—usually one curled up in my wife's lap. Do these sounds interrupt the silence? Of course. But in doing so, they highlight the silence the way an effective frame makes a work of art even more beautiful.

Embracing the contemplative life does not mean getting rid of noise or sound in your life. You can move to a remote wilderness area, but you will still encounter the symphony of nature or the intrusions of whatever sound your tools and belongings generate. Or you can be like me and decide that you like living in the city and that you still enjoy the blare of an electric guitar, even though you also have begun to hunger for contemplative silence and the still small voice of God. I mention this to highlight another danger into which people new to the contemplative life sometimes fall. If we turn our longing for the silence of God into a kind of witch hunt against the noises of our world, we risk limiting our spirituality in some sort of dualistic way, insisting that we find God only in quiet—and eventually coming to hate all forms of racket. But hate is not a fruit of the spirit; it is nothing more than the breakdown of love.

If you commit yourself to answering the contemplative call, you will eventually come to hunger for silence. Whether you are apophatic or kataphatic makes no difference, for either style of spirituality finds God in the silence. If you are like so many seekers, sooner or later you will try to make some real changes in your life to foster more silence, whether that is as simple as spending less time watching TV, or as dramatic as joining a monastery (or, like me, becoming spiritually associated with one). But no matter how much we do (or don't do) to change the circumstances of *external* noise in our lives, the mark of a healthy contemplative practice is how much attention we pay to cultivating *interior* silence. This will eventually transform how we relate, not only to silence, but to the sounds, wanted or unwanted, that continue to arise in our environment. Being a contemplative doesn't mean you'll never again listen to free jazz or heavy metal—nor will it protect you from the drone of a jetliner or the wail of a siren. But it will change *the way you listen* to these sounds, wanted or unwanted, that enter your ears.

Herein lies a paradox: contemplative silence is always with us, always bringing beauty into our lives, even when we ignore it or miss it because of how noisy we or our habitat have become. But once we learn to hear the whisper of this silence, we can begin to notice it *even in the noise*. That's not easy to do, of course, which is why most serious seekers of the contemplative life take at least some steps to reduce the overall decibel level in their environment. But while no one can have absolute control over the external noise in his or her world, everyone has the ability to seek, discern, and discover the silence within. And the more we get in touch with that inner world of wonders, the more we are able to pass through even the most cacophonous places outside of us.

Part of the contemplative call is an invitation to listen—for the silence hidden within the noise of our lives, within the internal as well as the external noise. When we listen, we are more available to discern the presence of the mystery of God, however it may come to us. We are more available to wake up. We are more disposed to receive the mystery of love and to be transformed by that mystery.

"Let all my world be silent in your presence, Lord, so that I may hear what the Lord God may say in my heart," wrote the twelfth-century Carthusian monk Guigo II. "Your words are so softly spoken that no one can hear them except in a deep silence. But to hear them lifts him who sits alone and in silence completely above his natural powers, because he who humbles himself will be lifted up. He who sits alone and listens will be raised above himself."[47]

So that's why, ultimately, contemplation is about silence. We enter silence to hear the silent voice of God. Yes, that sounds paradoxical. But no less a mystic than John of the Cross understood the relationship between the word and silence: "The Father spoke one Word, which was his Son, and this Word he speaks always in eternal silence, and in silence must it be heard by the soul."[48]

Behold!

"The fullness of joy is to behold God in everything," said Julian of Norwich.[49] This simple statement not only provides an important clue to the heart of mystical spirituality; it also points to the centrality of beholding as the essential contemplative practice. Our longing for God arises out of God's love for us—a love that beckons us to this fullness of joy, by inviting us to behold God in all.

John Skinner, who translated several mystical classics including Julian of Norwich's *Revelation of Love* into contemporary English, has this to say about beholding: "Perhaps the mental image to be conjured is a boy gazing with adoration across the room at the girl he knows loves him and she returning his glance with reciprocal love."[50] Beholding, in the mystical sense, is so much more than mere seeing or looking. It involves gazing, loving, receiving love, a sense of mutuality. We behold God in response to God beholding us. Maggie Ross, the Anglican solitary who has written eloquently on the centrality of beholding to the contemplative life, notes that "in our core silence, through our beholding, we realize our shared nature with God; we participate in the divine outpouring upon the world: incarnation, transfiguration and resurrection become conflated into a single movement of love."[51]

Ross also points out that, despite the fact that many modern translations of scripture have replaced the word *behold* with much more anemic words like *see* or even *remember*, both God's first word to humans (Genesis 1:29) and Jesus's last words to his disciples (Matthew 28:20) include the word *behold*. This is God's first and final call to us, the heart of the contemplative call: *Behold*. Behold God's presence in your life, whether seen or unseen, felt or unfelt, sensed or at a level deeper than sensation. Behold God's love for you, implicit in your desire for love and your ability to love, wounded and imperfect as it may be. Behold God's call—the very call summoning you to this intimate, transformed way of seeing. This call to behold is implicit in your awakening, no matter how subtle or dramatic your sense of being awakened may be. Even if you have no sense of being awakened, this call is yours. If you in any way long for God or God's blessing in your life, this call is hidden in the heart of your longing.

Beholding is about learning to see mindfully, to watch, to pay attention. One of the Desert Fathers—whose name is lost to us but who was thought to be named Macarius and so is known to us as "Pseudo-Macarius"—compared the act of beholding Christ to an artist's model holding his or her gaze steadily on the painter while the portrait is being made:

> Just as the portrait painter is attentive to the face of the king as he paints, and, when the face of the king is directly opposite, face to face, then he paints the portrait easily and well. But when he turns his face away, then the painter cannot paint because the face of the subject is not looking at the painter. In a similar way the good portrait painter, Christ, for those who believe in him and gaze continually toward him, at once paints according to his own

Answering the Contemplative Call

image a heavenly man. Out of his Spirit, out of the substance of the light itself, ineffable light, he paints a heavenly image . . . It is necessary that we gaze on him, believing and loving him, casting aside all else and attending to him so that he may paint his own heavenly image and send it into our souls. And thus carrying Christ, we may receive eternal life and even here, filled with confidence, we may be at rest.[52]

Pseudo-Macarius makes an important, vital point in this passage. Beholding God is an end unto itself. But, paradoxically, it is also a means to an end. In our beholding, we are transformed—we have the "heavenly image" of Christ engraved "into our souls." This becomes the key to eternal life, confidence, and rest. It is also the key to love and service, to giving away this transformation to those we are called to cherish and for whom we care.

There is a danger in all this talk about beholding that I feel needs to be addressed, however. Bear with me, for this is a bit of a mind-stretcher—a point that is difficult for us to wrap our minds around, because it runs so counter to the dogmas and beliefs and sacred cows of our postmodern, post-industrial, entertainment culture. *God is not an object.* Repeat: God is not an object. God is not a "thing" out there that you can see, the way you can go off and see the Eiffel Tower or the Great Wall of China. "Beholding God" is not just one more item on our heavenly to-do list that we can check off once we've done it. God is pure spirit, and has no anchored location in space and time. God is not an object because God is the ultimate *subject.* We human beings are always the objects of God's subjectivity, and not the other way around.

Now let's go even farther down the rabbit hole. Because God is not an object, it is absurd to talk about "experiencing God." Contemplation is not about us experiencing God; if anything, it is about God experiencing us.

Okay, I don't want to get too preachy here, so I'll admit that it's normal human nature for anyone interested in intimacy with God to talk about experiencing God. We all do it. I do it. This is how we have been trained to think. We think in terms of there being some sort of separation between humanity and God, and the way we bridge that divide is through the immediacy of experience. But beneath that "normal" way of thinking are some assumptions we have about God that aren't always useful or wise. For one thing, the idea that we are separate from God is itself an inaccurate assumption.

Furthermore, it is easy to assume that God-the-object exists to take care of us, in the same way that corn exists to feed us or water to slake our thirst. We think God exists to take care of us, to bless us, and—while few of us will admit it—we secretly think it's God's job to entertain us. Isn't this what mystical experience is all about? When people say, "I want to *experience* God," on one level, they are challenging the dogmas and unquestioned assumptions of generations of Christian teaching—basically saying, "I don't want to accept what someone else says is true about God; I want to see for myself." I can respect the healthy skepticism that propels such a desire for direct union with God. But then what happens is that we default to our cultural programming, and we look for God to give us an "experience of God," which can mean anything from a warm fuzzy feeling to a mind-blowing, mind-expanding Buddha-like mystical encounter worthy of George Lucas's special-effects team. We figure that God is better than LSD, and so we expect that a true mystical experience will fry our circuits better than the best acid.

But all of this is based on the idea that God is an object, that we are the subjects, that we are running the show here, and that God's job is to show up when we call and give us the celestial fireworks, neatly packaged within the theater found inside our skulls.

By the grace of God, it doesn't work that way.

Anything we say about God quickly unfolds into a paradox. This can be seen in the Christian teaching about the Trinity—the recognition that God is One, singularity, perfect simplicity. And yet in this oneness, God includes three persons: Father, Son, and Holy Spirit. There is no logic to explain this neatly away. Of course, theologians with minds far greater than mine have tried. Others, perhaps getting a little closer to the heart of things, have compared the doctrine of the Trinity to a Zen *koan*—a logic buster of an assertion that is designed to help spring human consciousness from the trap of dualistic thinking. What is more important than trying to figure out the Trinity (or walking away from it, dismissing it as absurd), however, is recognizing that everything we say about God quickly reveals yet another paradox. Call God "creator," but then what do we make of the fact that destruction is a part of every creative act? Call God "Father," but then wrestle with the fact that this image of a loving parent can lead to sexist assumptions about God (and humanity).[53] Then there's the classic atheist's complaint: if God is all good and all powerful, why does God permit horrific injustice and evil to persist in the world?

Even the statement that I believe is the best affirmation we can make about God—"God is love"—ultimately fails. It fails because it is conditioned by human, mortal, dualistic understandings of love. Since we can't get out of the box of what it means to be mortal, finite, imperfect flesh-and-blood creatures no matter how far we try to stretch our understanding of love in order to get a sense of God, we end up just reducing God in our minds to our limited ideas about love—rather than having our notions of love expanded and divinized by God. Even the most brilliant minds and the most loving hearts can hold only a human-sized caricature of God, a badly rendered image of what God truly is. Whatever reveals God conceals God. (As you read this paragraph, I hope you kept in mind the tension between kataphatic and apophatic approaches to God, for that tension dances all through my line of thinking here.)

God is not an object out there that exists for the benefit of our experience in here. That's not to say that people can't and don't undergo countless wondrous, extraordinary encounters that only seem to make sense when understood as dramatic evidence of the presence of God in their lives. Yes, that happens, all the time. But to say, "I want to experience God," is rather like saying, "I want to understand love." To understand love, find someone to love, and love him or her. To *really* understand love, find someone unlovable to love, or someone who is incapable of loving you back. Experiencing God works the same way. If you want to encounter God, then listen to Julian of Norwich and seek to behold God in everything. Don't bother looking for God. Take a deep breath and relax into your longing, and remember that it is a mirror. God is looking for you.

So just how *do* you behold God in everything? Here's where all the language and stories and teachings of the Christian wisdom tradition help us. The tradition affirms that God is omnipresent—which means God is everywhere, which means God is in everything, and you didn't have a thing to do with it. God lives in you; God is the source of your being, your life. Yet God is out of control—that is to say, outside your control—and God is hidden in plain sight. God is gazing at you, beholding you, right here, right now. Never mind what you feel or don't feel, perceive or don't perceive. If you are experiencing God this very moment, a moment from now you can easily fill your mind with doubts. Who's to say it isn't just your imagination or some sort of psychological quirk—a flood of endorphins in your brain chemistry? But turn this around. If you are *not* experiencing God, perhaps *that* is just a psychological quirk or an anomaly in your brain chemistry. Carl Jung said: "Bidden or not bidden, God is present." Experienced or not experienced, God is present. Beheld or not beheld, God is.

Here's another *koan* to chew on. Perhaps any effort we expend on trying to behold this hidden God will simply send us scurrying off in the wrong direction. The more you try to behold God, the more you end up merely beholding your efforts to behold God. The more you talk about God, the more your mind gets wrapped up in your clever thoughts and educated opinions. C. S. Lewis has some funny things to say about this in his novel *The Great Divorce*, about heaven and hell. Hell, it seems, has plenty of eminent philosophers and theologians in it, who spend all of eternity arguing with each other about how their particular way of talking about God is the "right" way. And all of them have missed the point.[54]

There's a Zen saying I find useful when considering the paradox of beholding: "Quit trying. Quit trying not to try. Quit quitting." If you want to behold God in everything, don't *try* to behold God in everything (or anything), but don't *not try* either. Consider this: beholding God in everything is our natural state of being. So the trick is to unlearn all the ways we keep ourselves from beholding God. And that has a lot to do with learning how to shut up or at least slow down the internal chatter and commentary—the monkey mind that keeps intruding on your efforts to be silent. Beholding is linked to that open, spacious moment between the time we wake up and the time we kick our normal, gotta-stay-in-charge selves (i.e., our thinking, chattering, distracted monkey minds) into gear. That open, spacious place is not just something that happens at the moment when we first wake up. It is with us at all times. It usually seems, however, that we are too busy chattering with ourselves, or trying to maintain or assert control over our lives, to notice. It is scary even to consider surrendering our efforts to control our lives; yet if we can loosen the grip and relax into the awareness of the present moment with a humble and loving heart—then, by grace, we may join Julian of Norwich in beholding God in all.

Worship

"**W**e become what we do," proclaimed the twentieth century Quaker contemplative Douglas V. Steere. "A great religious interpreter of our times once said that he kissed his child because he loved her and that he kissed his child in order to love her more." In other words, love is a commitment, not just a feeling. And it is in showing that commitment to love that we slowly, over time, become loving beings. Steere's point is not just to affirm human love, however. He wants us to consider the ramifications in regard to our relationship with God. He goes on to say: "Regular participation in corporate worship is a school and a workshop in which those who would grow in the religious life, no matter how tenuous may be their present connections, should be in attendance."[55]

If you're not familiar with the term *corporate worship*, it does not mean bowing down before Exxon, General Electric, or Toyota. Nor does it mean adoring the human body. Steere refers to the gathering together of people for the purpose of worshipping God. Maybe a better way to describe this is as *communal* worship—gathering in a community for the purpose of adoring, loving, and praising the Divine mystery—not in opposition to prayer, meditation, and contemplation as solitary endeavors, but rather as an important complement to these private practices.

For two millennia, the contemplatives and mystics of the Christian tradition have included communal worship in their practice of spirituality. The Rule of Saint Benedict, the document by which most monasteries have been governed for almost 1,500 years, devotes chapter after chapter to describing meticulously what the daily worship routine for monks should be like. Over a thousand years later, the Russian mystical tale *The Way of a Pilgrim* follows the adventure of a solitary traveler journeying through the countryside and practicing the presence of God by continually reciting a simple prayer. But whenever he gets a chance, this homeless pilgrim eagerly joins with others in either praying together or participating in the liturgy at a nearby Church or monastery. Evelyn Underhill, who became renowned for her writings on mysticism, made worship the focus of her last major book, which was published shortly before her death. In fact, her two most important books were each published with a single-word title: *Mysticism* and *Worship*. And pretty much all the great mystics—from Meister Eckhart, to John of the Cross, to Thomas Merton—assume that serious seekers after God sustain their journeys with serious, ongoing immersion in the life of communal praise, adoration, and reception of the sacraments.

I subscribe to what Brian McLaren calls "a generous orthodoxy," meaning that, like C. S. Lewis and others before me, I'm not going to make a case for any one particular denomination within the universal Christian faith. Jesus said: "For where two or three are gathered in my name, I am there among them" (Matthew 18:20). With that in mind, I *am* going to insist that participating in corporate worship *in some form* is an essential step in following the mystical path.

Communal worship can take many forms. At its minimum, it entails two or three (or more) folks gathering together for shared prayer (spoken, silent, and/or sung), along with reading and reflecting on the words of sacred scripture. Such informal gatherings often occur in people's homes or in small group settings, whether at churches or other locations. Indeed, many Christians prefer to participate in "house churches," faith communities that, by design, are small enough to meet in people's homes and often do not have paid clergy. Of course, the most typical form of Church is the local parish, whatever its denomination: Orthodox, Catholic, Episcopal, Lutheran, Methodist, and Presbyterian, among others. Among these different churches, you can find a wide variety of worship styles—from the highly stylized, ritualistic ceremonies of Catholic and Orthodox churches, to the free-form prayer-and-praise meetings of many evangelical churches. Perhaps the most minimalist of all styles of worship is that of the "un-programmed" meetings of Quakers (Friends), who sit in meditative silence for an hour, mostly silent except when a participant feels led by the Spirit to speak briefly.

Jesus may have suggested that "two or three" is a quorum for his presence, but he never gave an upper limit to that number. In our day, you can find plenty of opportunities to worship with literally thousands (or tens of thousands) of people, from papal Masses, to revivals or Christian music festivals, to mega-churches in which popular or charismatic evangelists minister to huge congregations.

For the most part, unless you live in such a small and remote community that you simply don't have access to many options, you probably have a wide variety of worship opportunities available to you.

Pick the size of community with which you are comfortable and the style of worship that nurtures you, and go with it. What's important here is that you balance your individual efforts to respond to God with time spent worshipping God with others.

What is worship, anyway? The word, as defined in the *Oxford English Dictionary*, has a much broader sense than merely praising and adoring God. Historically, it has been applied to *anyone*, God or human, who is worthy of praise, honor, or esteem. To this day, "Your

Answering the Contemplative Call

Worship" is a title in British Commonwealth countries for a magistrate. Within a spiritual context, worship is whatever we do to bless, honor, praise, or express our esteem for and devotion to God. Therefore, communal worship entails having the guts to stand up before (or alongside) others and offer praise or honor to God in a public, or at least semi-public, forum.

There is a strong countercultural component here, on two levels. Our society (I'm speaking specifically as an American here, although I suspect this will apply to many other societies around the globe as well) is fiercely individualistic, which means we resist showing deference to anyone—to other human beings as well as to God. But it also means that we assume that spirituality is like sex—meant to be private, not really appropriate for public display. Indeed, some Christians point to Matthew 6:1 as evidence that Jesus was opposed to public worship, even though the verse, when read in context, has nothing to do with communal worship, but rather is clearly criticizing public displays of charity.

Perhaps our resistance to communal worship would lose weight, however, if we thought of Christianity—including the contemplative and mystical dimensions of Christian spirituality—as essentially *social* and *relational* in nature, rather than as *individualistic,* as our secular society has become. I'm not saying that Christianity is anti-individualist (far from it), only that the Christian wisdom tradition historically has balanced the needs of the individual with the concerns of the community as a whole. As Kenneth Leech points out, in commenting on the Trinitarian nature of God: "In God there is social life, community, sharing. To share in God is to share in that life."[56] When we worship with others, we love our neighbors while simultaneously loving God. That may seem to be a stretch, but consider that, when you participate in communal worship, you support others who are there seeking to find a closer connection to God. No matter how slight it may be, your mere presence in such a setting is a loving act.

How, then, do we worship God? How do we honor or esteem the Divine mystery? This can take many forms, some of which are also appropriate for private practice. We pray, either using formal language ("liturgy") or, when appropriate, forming our prayers in our own words. Many worship services also include some silent time for prayers offered within the privacy of our inner thoughts. Communal worship also offers the opportunity to sing our prayers, joining our voices together in a corporate harmony of praise. As Saint Augustine notes, those who sing their prayers are, in effect, "praying twice."

Communal worship also entails the reading of scripture (or listening to others as they read), with sermons or discussions designed to help us meditate and reflect on the text's meaning. Many worship services also have an element of sacrifice built in—an opportunity to make offerings of money or sometimes even other items, to be gathered by the community leadership and dispersed where needed. In some churches, this gesture of offering is ritually linked to Holy Communion (also known as the Eucharist, the Lord's Supper, the Blessed Sacrament)—the ceremonial meal shared together in response to Christ's instructions to "do this in remembrance of me," as recorded in the New Testament. Without wanting to get into the various and conflicting ways that different Christian groups have understood Communion over the years, I think we can confidently say that, across the board, it represents an act of devotion and worship centered on the mysterious Biblical phrases "this is my body" and "this is my blood." After all, Jesus said: "If you love me, you will keep my commandments" (John 14:15). And praying to God, worshipping God, receiving Communion, and, most important of all, loving one another are some of the ways Christians can keep the commandments of Jesus.

Worship wonderfully invites us to integrate the head and the heart in our quest for deeper intimacy with God. Worship can be very mentally stimulating, with devotional language, scripture passages, and opportunities for personal reflection that help us to hone our mental, cognitive efforts to know God as best we can. But more than this, worship is a matter of the heart. It can be deeply emotionally satisfying, helping to stimulate feelings of love and devotion that can strengthen our sense of intimacy with God (or, at least, longing for that intimacy). Saint Bernard of Clairvaux understood this emotional dimension of worship, and recognized that it can be a doorway into profound contemplation.

> As a drop of water seems to disappear completely in a big quantity of wine, even assuming the wine's taste and color; just as red, molten iron becomes so much like fire it seems to lose its primary state; just as the air on a sunny day seems transformed into sunshine instead of being lit up; so it is necessary for the saints that all human feelings melt in a mysterious way and flow into the will of God.[57]

In worship, we are that drop of water; God is the wine. We are the molecules of air that are shot through with the omnipresent light of God. When we worship, we not only have the opportunity to cultivate profound feelings of love and devotion; we can also offer those feelings, along with the emotions of all those who join us in worship, to God.

As I've already said, this emphasis on the social, communal act of corporate worship is not meant to suggest that Christian spirituality has no place for private meditation and contemplation. On the contrary, like all forms of mystical spirituality, Christian contemplation emphasizes the power of seeking intimacy with God in silence and solitude. But this is not an either/or choice. Communal worship supports these interior efforts. Both are necessary for a balanced spiritual diet.

The Other Side of Worship

I took pains in the preceding chapter to emphasize the role of communal worship in the Christian life for a simple reason: those who are drawn to contemplation (and I speak very much from personal experience here) are often introverts, or at the very least have their own reasons for preferring a private spiritual practice to a corporate gathering. But even contemplatives need to get outside of their comfort zone. If you feel drawn to private prayer, but dislike praying with others, sooner or later your journey of growth in the Spirit will include a call to communal prayer—if for no other reason than the sake of discovering the relational dimension of prayer.

For some people, however, the opposite situation is true. They feel comfortable participating in a public Sunday morning Church service, but resist any efforts to pray in solitude or secrecy. Such resistance may be active ("I don't like to pray alone; it makes me feel embarrassed") or passive ("Gee, I'm so busy; I never find the time to pray"). But such excuses will not let them off the hook—for hidden, intimate prayer, alone with God, is truly the other side of worship, as important to spiritual growth as any communal act of devotion. We are called into the prayer of solitude as surely as we are called into communal forms of worship. Jesus stated it bluntly in the Sermon on the Mount, when he instructed his listeners to "pray in secret" (Matthew 6:6). Such solitary prayer, which can take a number of forms, is the heart of contemplative practice—the lifeblood of mystical spirituality.

In the 1980s, ethnologist Michael Harner popularized a concept called "core shamanism," based on the idea that, by studying the wisdom of different shamans and other healers from indigenous cultures around the world, scholars and practitioners could identify key beliefs and practices that represent the core of shamanic wisdom. Although this approach to indigenous wisdom is not without its critics, it has proven to be a popular way for people who are drawn to shamanic practice, but who are not themselves part of indigenous cultures and therefore have no access to shamanic teachers, to learn about shamanism and to apply its wisdom to their own lives.

It seems to me that Christian contemplation and shamanism have a similar dynamic in terms of how their respective wisdom is being disseminated in today's world. Shamanism is the healing practice of indigenous cultures—cultures that, alas, are rapidly vanishing or being assimilated into neighboring agricultural, industrial, or post-industrial societies. While core shamanism may not be a perfect way to understand and enter into the wisdom of the shamans of the world, it nevertheless has helped to ensure that shamanic practices are studied, practiced, and appreciated in the post-indigenous cultures of the world, hopefully for generations to come.

For the Christian mystical tradition, the "indigenous culture" is found in monasteries, convents, friaries, and hermitages. Ever since the Desert Fathers and Mothers organized the earliest monasteries back in the third and fourth centuries, these Christian intentional communities have been the epicenter of contemplative practice. After over 1,500 years, however, the dynamic of spirituality within Christianity is changing rapidly. Especially in the West, Christian monasticism faces an uncertain future, as fewer men and women enter into consecrated life. Existing monasteries and convents often struggle because of aging and declining membership as well as changing economic realities. Monasteries that functioned as working farms fifty years ago today often face the same financial problems as any other family farm, only with fewer young workers to take on the challenge. Even the monasteries that are surviving are finding that their culture is rapidly changing, as they rely on new ways of making a living—from manufacturing to retail sales to providing hospitality to guests. These changes often impact the delicate ecosystem of the contemplative life in unforeseen ways.

As social, cultural, and economic changes impact the monasteries, their traditional role as guardians of Christian wisdom will no doubt evolve and change. What is interesting—and, I would say, providential—is that precisely at this point in history, as the old culture of monasticism is changing forever, the hunger for contemplative spirituality among people *outside* of monasteries and convents is greater than ever. Monks and nuns are discovering that, even though fewer people actually want to join their communities, more people than ever are hoping to learn from them, taking the wisdom that has been honed and refined for centuries behind cloister walls and applying it to the challenges and realities of urban and suburban life.

Walter Hilton, one of the great medieval English mystics, wrote *The Mixed Life*, an important treatise providing spiritual direction for individuals with family and career responsibilities that prevented them from entering the cloister. But, while the roots of this movement toward lay contemplative practice go back to the fourteenth century, the twentieth and twenty-first centuries have really become the age of "the mystical way in everyday life"[58]—the spirituality of those who are drawn toward a deep, profound, transformational life in silence, meditation, prayer, and contemplation, even while having to integrate that call into all the other demands of a secular life and career, relationships with family and friends, and other self-directed pursuits.

By the grace of God, I pray that monasteries and other religious communities will always be with us, as beacons of hope and contemplative silence in our increasingly noisy and distracted world. It seems, however, that, just as Michael Harner and his associates helped to bring shamanism out of its remote indigenous setting into the spiritual hunger of the postmodern world, so it is our task to discover the heart of monastic wisdom today and relate it to the needs and longings of society at large. With this in mind, I would like to propose the concept of *core contemplation,* in essence distilling the teachings of great mystics from the time of the Desert Fathers and Mothers up to the present day into a basic spiritual practice that any Christian can incorporate into his or her life of solitary prayer.

Evelyn Underhill advocated a "practical mysticism" for "normal people" (by which she meant, not people who aren't abnormal, but laypersons—people who aren't priests or nuns or monks). Thomas Merton recognized that *le point vierge*—the point where humanity accesses the presence of God—is in everybody, not just monks or nuns. And of course, the great Jesuit theologian Karl Rahner said: "The Christian of the future will be a mystic or . . . will not exist at all." I believe these great mystics of the twentieth century all came to the same conclusion—that when even the most ordinary and down to earth people embrace the core mystical practices, they don't merely become devout or pious; they truly become contemplatives, mystics, in the world. In other words, the fullness of mystical spirituality—of the call of Divine love and the promise of union with God—is now available to everyone, and these core mystical practices are one way to open our hearts to receive the fullness of Divine blessing.

Notice that I didn't say "the core mystical practices will make us have mystical experiences." Mystical practices *dispose* us to receive the blessings of intimacy with God, which can take an infinite variety of forms. God's presence in our lives is always, to some degree, hidden, which means it is always, to some degree, *mystical*—whether or not we feel or perceive or recognize anything we may describe as "mystical."

For this reason, at the risk of being overly cautious, I want to I stress that just beginning to practice a form of contemplative prayer does not automatically entitle us to call ourselves "mystics." Despite (or, perhaps, because of) what Rahner said, I believe Christians should always be extremely humble when it comes to describing themselves as mystics. There are several reasons for this. First, we must always remember that mystical prayer, mystical consciousness, and mystical union are always freely given gifts from God. We cannot earn, or presume to deserve, such grace.

Second, I think that there is great danger in ego inflation when it comes to spiritual practices. If we are not careful, we run the risk of using "mysticism" or "being a mystic" as a way of embracing spiritual narcissism, rather than the more truly mystical path of spiritual *kenosis* (a topic we will explore in a forthcoming chapter). Here's the paradox in a nutshell: one of the signs of being a true mystic is *forgetting about yourself* in the joy of loving and being loved by God. Conversely, if we get too caught up on how "advanced"[59] we are in the spiritual life, or whether we deserve to be called "mystics" or not, it seems that we spend too much time *thinking about ourselves* rather than simply getting on with the business of intimacy with God.

The importance of self-forgetfulness is another clue as to why the practice of contemplative Christianity must always be embedded in community. No matter how strongly you feel called to a life of profound silence and solitude, it needs to be grounded in some form of relatedness with others, for the sake of love, of accountability, and of service.

As Christians, we are called to love our neighbors as ourselves. This is not negotiable. If we retreat into a real or psychological solitude that cuts off from others, we are no longer truly walking in the path of Jesus. Even the great hermits of the deserts in the fourth century occasionally met for communal worship. And, of course, they were the forefathers and foremothers of the monasteries, which were modeled as communities of faith. Moreover, central to love is service (which can be defined as "love made visible"). "If we live in solitude, whose feet shall we wash?" asked one of the wiser Desert Fathers, and that question remains just as relevant today. Jesus insisted that, "whatever you do to the least of these (i.e., those who are in need), you do to me." In other words, by serving others, we grow in our love for Christ.

Finally, community is necessary because we human beings need to be accountable to one another. We need others to call us out on all the subtle and not-so-subtle ways in which we try to deceive ourselves. This is rarely fun, and often quite painful. But if we are serious about growth in the love of Christ (and each other), accountability is a necessary part of the process.

So, recognizing the humility of not focusing on how mystical we are, and appreciating that Christian contemplation is always embedded in concentric circles of community, here are the core spiritual practices of the Christian wisdom tradition: meditation and contemplative (silent) prayer. The journey into the mystery of God is a journey into these two essential mystical practices.

Of Word and Image— Christian Meditation

T o someone unfamiliar with the history of Christian spirituality, *meditation* is a word that typically evokes Eastern spiritual
practices like Zazen, Samatha, or Vipassanā. These practices
are techniques for cultivating attention, relaxation, insight, or mental
clarity. They are not necessarily *spiritual*, in the sense of seeking or
finding intimacy with God or any other spiritual entity. They are, in
essence, exercises for improving mental fitness.

While these exercises are what most people think of when they
use the word *meditation*, Christian meditation has traditionally had a
more specific meaning, related to the history of the word itself. Meditation is derived from the Greek word *medesthai*, which means "to
think about" or "to care for"—carrying even the connotation of turning a thought over in the mind, almost as if to examine it from every
angle. Unlike the Eastern idea of meditation as a desired state of mental peace and clarity, the Christian idea of meditation is much more
interactive, allowing the mind (and heart) to engage with the object of
meditation—God, Christ, the Spirit, the Trinity, the Divine mystery.

So Christian meditation is not about letting images or thoughts go; rather, like other forms of kataphatic spirituality, it is all about immersing ourselves in the Word of God.

"In the beginning was the Word," begins the Gospel of John. And ever since the apostles wrote the New Testament epistles and the evangelists wrote the Gospels, the Christian wisdom tradition has been associated with the mysteries of language. We use words to pray, to communicate with one another, to express love and longing, to offer blessings, and to confess wrongdoing. It is by our words that we teach our children, comfort the afflicted, and speak out against injustice. We tell stories to one another to learn, to grow, to resolve conflicts, and to maintain identity.

To use language is an essential part of being human, and so the exploration of Christian wisdom includes a strong focus on the words of the first Christian teachers, as well as of the great saints and mystics throughout history. So meditation is not a means to *break away* from the words of the Bible or the liturgy or the teachings of the saints and the mystics—or, for that matter, even the words of our own thoughts. Rather, Christian meditation entails a *reflection* on those treasures and functions as a bridge between the words and images of earthly spirituality and the eventual letting-go of such spiritual material into the silent mystery of contemplation.

Henri Nouwen understood the basic goodness of mental activity—of thoughts, imagination, and feelings—that forms the basis of Christian meditation in all its kataphatic splendor. As he pointed out:

> Our minds are always active. We analyze, reflect, daydream, or dream. There is not a moment during the day or night when we are not thinking. You might say our thinking is "unceasing." Sometimes we wish that we could stop thinking for a while; that would save us from many worries, guilt feelings, and fears. Our ability to think is our greatest gift, but it is also the source of our

greatest pain. Do we have to become victims of our unceasing thoughts? No, we can convert our unceasing thinking into unceasing prayer by making our inner monologue into a continuing dialogue with our God, who is the source of all love. Let's break out of our isolation and realize that Someone who dwells in the center of our beings wants to listen with love to all that occupies and preoccupies our minds.[60]

Indeed, his advice is to recognize that any inner process, no matter how mundane, can be a portal into meditation and prayer.

Saint John of the Cross understood the heart of spiritual practice and expressed it in a pithy saying: "Seek in reading and you will find in meditation; knock in prayer and it will be opened to you in contemplation."[61] The words of spiritual guidance and insight we encounter when we read (or when we pray in a formal manner, using the kinds of prayers that are found in books) are words that invite us into meditation, which in turn can lead to spontaneous prayer, which in turn shades off into contemplation.

Walter Hilton, likewise, notes: "There are three means most commonly used by people who devote themselves to contemplation: the reading of holy scripture and of holy teaching, spiritual meditation, and diligent prayer with devotion."[62] Both Hilton and John of the Cross are referring to an ancient monastic practice called *lectio divina* (Latin for "sacred reading"). *Lectio* entails a particular approach to the sacred writings of the Christian tradition. Most Christians are familiar with the concept of Bible study, but that suggests reading the Bible like a textbook, seeking intellectual knowledge to forge a deeper understanding of the history, theology, and ethics of Christianity. This is a fine thing to do. But *lectio* implies a more spiritual, heart-centered approach to reading the Bible or other sacred texts. As described in the writings of the medieval monk Guigo II, *lectio* involves four essential steps:

- *Read* the Bible (or other spiritual text) slowly, meditatively, while pondering what unique and personal message God may have *for you* in the text you are reading. Read the text the way you would read a letter from a dear, cherished friend: savor every single word and phrase.

- *Reflect* on how the text and its meaning impact you. Does it make you feel inspired? Convinced? Bored? Challenged? Confused? Angry? Joyful? Reflect on how you react to the words you've read, for your reaction is a clue to the spiritual gift(s) the text has to offer you.

- *Respond* to the words you've read. This is your opportunity to open your heart and mind to God, trusting in God's presence even if you don't feel it. Such a response traditionally is put into words—your own words, prayerfully offered to God. You can simply pray, or write in a journal, or even try a more creative way of responding, like sketching or drawing your response.

- *Rest* in God's presence, whether felt or hidden inside you. Each of the three prior steps points toward this final act. Here you give up any effort to understand what you've read or how you respond. There's no need to impress God or strive for any special insight or understanding. You rest as a small baby rests— serenely in its mother's arms.

In Part Two, I commended the importance of doing your research before taking a trip. *Lectio* builds on that basic idea—that spirituality is something worth exploring by getting to know the words and teachings of wise elders who came before us. But more than just teaching you the mental concepts necessary to comprehend theology, *lectio* invites you into the heart of these words of wisdom through the practice of meditation—the inner process of reflecting on the wisdom.

Meditation, obviously, involves turning inward. "There are eyes deeper within than the eyes, and a hearing deeper within this hearing," notes Pseudo-Macarius.

> As these eyes sensibly behold and recognize the face of a friend or beloved one, so the eyes of the worthy and faithful soul, being spiritually enlightened with the light of God, behold and recognize the true Friend, the sweetest and greatly longed for Bridegroom, the Lord, while the soul is shone upon by the adorable Spirit; and thus beholding . . . the desirable and only inexpressible beauty, it is smitten with passionate love for God, and is directed to all virtues of the Spirit.[63]

In other words, meditating on Christ, on the Spirit, on the triune God, are means by which we behold the beauty and glory of the Divine mystery. And in that beholding, we are invited into ever-deeper love and intimacy with God.

One of the great teachers of Christian meditation was Ignatius of Loyola, sixteenth-century Spanish mystic and the founder of the Jesuits. In his classic retreat manual, *The Spiritual Exercises*, he provides detailed instructions on using the imagination and memory to create vivid interior visualizations of events from the life of Christ, like his preaching ministry or the Last Supper. Ignatius recommends making this inner, imaginary tableau as lifelike as possible—to "see" in your mind's eye the road from Bethany to Jerusalem or the room where the supper took place.[64] Ignatius understood that the more vivid the meditative exercise, the more powerful its impact on your soul. Of course, it doesn't stop with visualizing the environment. The imaginal experience included seeing Jesus, watching him as he preached or washed his disciples' feet or shared the bread and wine of the Last Supper.

From there, the purpose of meditation is to recognize the depth and quality of your response to Jesus. Do you feel loving? Indifferent? Devoted? Bored? To take an exercise like this a step beyond Ignatius, what would it look like to immerse your sense of longing for God into this meditative encounter with Christ? What can you imagine Christ saying to you, if you were present with him during his earthly life? Can you imagine what he might say to you now, addressing your needs and the blind spots in your life today? Questions like these point to the rich possibilities that present themselves to us as we enter into a meditative encounter with Christ.

After immersing ourselves in the Word given to us through scripture or other sacred writings, and reflecting on that Word through the inner art of meditation, the traditional third step of *lectio divina* involves responding, or informal prayer. I think of this stage as the last step on the road to the deep silence of contemplation. It's an opportunity to acknowledge whatever thoughts or feelings may be lurking in you—especially in regard to the reading or meditation, but also in relation to anything else that may be going on in your life. Obviously, such a step is taken more for our own benefit than for God's, who naturally does not need to be told what is going on in our hearts and minds.

We sometimes need to take a moment to acknowledge for ourselves what is going on, however. Such an act of prayer can be profoundly relaxing, and perhaps even a source of healing in our lives. It can also be a way to anchor yourself in God's presence (whether or not you feel it)—and even a way of recognizing a deeper connection with other human beings, as Thomas Merton once noted.

> If I am going to pray validly and deeply, it will be with a consciousness of myself as being more than just myself when I pray. In other words, I am not just an individual when I pray, and I am not just an individual with grace when I pray. When I pray, I am in a certain sense, everybody. The mind that prays in me is more than my own mind, and the thoughts that come up in me are more than my own thoughts because this deep consciousness

when I pray is a place of encounter between myself and God and between the common love of everybody. It is the common will and love of the Church meeting with my will and God's will in my consciousness and conscience when I pray.[65]

Perhaps such a profound insight into the transpersonal dimensions of prayer will not be a conscious part of every act of prayer. But whether we feel it or not, we can affirm that, on a level deeper than conscious awareness, prayer makes this kind of unity real. Julian of Norwich said it far more simply still: "Prayer makes the soul one with God."[66]

Walter Hilton saw prayer as a *sacramental* act—in other words, as a channel through which the grace of God flows into our lives.

> The purpose of prayer is to make you ready and able to receive as a clean vessel the grace that our Lord would freely give to you. . . . For though it is true that prayer is not the cause of our Lord's grace being given, it is nevertheless a channel by which that grace freely flows into a soul.[67]

Our prayers can be profoundly simple, perhaps as bluntly candid as "I'm scared, I'm lonely, and I'm tired." Sometimes our prayers amount to little more than self-involved wish lists, complaining to God about all the things we lack in our lives. It is okay to pray such prayers (after all, we may as well be honest in our prayer), but it is also important to open up to the possibility of a deeper level of prayer—one that emerges, not out of our neediness, but out of our desire and love for God. Such deeper prayers are the ones that truly take flight. Consider this prayer, from the fourteenth-century Italian mystic Catherine of Siena:

> Eternal Trinity, you are my creator and I am the work of your hands. I know, through the new creation which you have given me in the blood of Christ, that you are enamored of the beauty of your workmanship. Oh, Abyss! Oh, Eternal Godhead! Oh, Sea Profound! What more could you give me than yourself? You are

Answering the Contemplative Call

the fire that always burns without being consumed; you consume in your heart all the soul's self-love; you are the fire which takes away all cold; with your light you illuminate me so that I may know the fullness of your truth. You are the light above all light which mystically illuminates the eye of my mind, clarifying the light of faith so abundantly and so perfectly that I may see the life of my soul, and in this light receive you—the true light.[68]

Granted, these are the words of a mystical master, and comparing our feeble attempts at prayer to them is like comparing a child's first efforts at playing the piano to the virtuosity of Vladimir Horowitz or Martha Argerich. Don't worry if your words are simple and unadorned. God wants *you*, not your literary flair.

Finally, however, there comes a point when the natural chattiness of our inner voices needs to settle down and be quiet. This point is the threshold of contemplation.

Praying the Silence

The contemplative call invites us to the mystery of "Christ in you" (Colossians 1:27). We respond to this call through contemplative prayer. Thus, contemplation is a central part of Christian spirituality—a core mystical practice. It is a topic many mystics explored in their writings. Consider what Teresa of Avila, Thomas Merton, and Evelyn Underhill have said about it.

Teresa of Avila advises us thus:

> Let it [your soul] try, without forcing itself or causing any turmoil, to put a stop to all discursive reasoning, yet not to suspend the understanding, nor to cease from all thought, though it is well for it to remember that it is in God's presence and Who this God is. If feeling this should lead it into a state of absorption, well and good, but it should not try to understand what this state is, because that is a gift bestowed upon the will. The will, then, should be left to enjoy it, and should not labor except for uttering a few loving words, for although in such a case one may not

INVOICE

One Spirit

| ACCOUNT NUMBER | 077411143 | FEBRUARY 19 2013 | ORDER NUMBER 092 | INVOICE NUMBER 56793472 |

DESCRIPTION	ITEM NO.	TYPE	ITEM STATUS	PUB PRICE	YOUR PRICE
CONTMPLTV CALL	13-716636	Bonus Pt	Enclosed	16.95	4.99

Thank you for your order!

- You saved $11.96 on this shipment.
- Get $10 CASH BACK! Go to RebateClaim.com

SUBTOTAL	4.99
SHIPPING & HANDLING	3.99
TAX	.00
SHIPMENT TOTAL	8.98
PREVIOUS BALANCE	.00
TOTAL DUE	**$.00**

For Customer Service:
Call: **1-717-918-2665**

Web: www.onespirit.com

TO MAKE A PAYMENT

- BY PHONE: Call toll-free to make an automated payment: (888) 954-2665.

- BY MAIL: Detach bottom portion, and place this invoice plus payment in envelope with address showing through the window and proper postage affixed.

- **DO NOT send returns to the payment address or by using the payment invoice. Returns are not processed at this location. See "RETURNS" section for proper information.**

DO NOT write comments on payment form as they cannot be processed on these forms! Please use above contact methods for comments / customer service inquiries.

RETURN INSTRUCTIONS

- Write what you are returning on the front side of this form. Do not send any payment with a return.

- Place form on top of returned items in the package/box; do not put form inside any books.

- Affix postage and mail to:

  Product Return Center
  Hanover, PA 17332

DO NOT send returns to the Payment Processing Center address! They will not be processed at this location.

Be sure to write your account number on all payments, correspondence, and returns.

Please allow 2 weeks after mailing for payments and 4 weeks for returns to be processed and posted to your account.

Credit/Debit Card Convenience

When you authorize us to use your credit or debit card for all future orders and charges, we will automatically charge the card you provide for all orders and other charges related to your membership. This includes shipments of Featured Selections unless otherwise noted (see Membership Agreement). If applicable, your card may be charged at the end of your commitment period for any remaining selections required to complete your purchase commitment. We will continue to charge the card you provide unless you notify us of a change. In the event your card is no longer active (for example, the card has expired or we cannot obtain authorization from your card issuer), for your convenience we will attempt to charge any other card that you have placed on file with us, in order to prevent disruption of your membership. To change credit or debit card to be used for your club account, simply contact Customer Service.

QUESTIONS ABOUT YOUR ORDER?

Please email us at:
questions@memberservice.com

Or write to us at:

Customer Service
PO Box 916400
Rantoul, IL 61866-6400

Or call us at the customer service phone number listed on the front of this form.

be striving to cease from thought, such cessation often comes, though for a very short time.[69]

For another perspective, it is perhaps not surprising that Thomas Merton, as a Trappist monk, understood contemplation in terms that seem austere:

> Contemplative prayer is, in a way, simply the preference for the desert, for emptiness, for poverty. One has begun to know the meaning of contemplation when he intuitively and spontaneously seeks the dark and unknown path of aridity in preference to every other way. The contemplative is one who would rather not know than know. Rather not enjoy than enjoy. Rather not have proof that God loves him. He accepts the love of God on faith, in defiance of all apparent evidence.[70]

Meanwhile, Evelyn Underhill saw an essential link between contemplation and humility (self-forgetfulness):

> The condition of all valid seeing and hearing, upon every plane of consciousness, lies not in the sharpening of the senses, but in a peculiar attitude of the whole personality: in a self-forgetting attentiveness, a profound concentration, a self-merging, which operates a real communion between the seer and the seen—in a word, in Contemplation.[71]

In the beginning was the Word: but words require a backdrop of silence—or, at least, relative quiet—in order to be heard. Speak to someone standing in front of a jet engine or some other noisemaker, and both you and your listener will be frustrated. God's Word emerged out of "the sound of sheer silence" (I Kings 19:12), and words of the Divine mystery have been emerging out of silence ever since. To pray in silence is to surrender the noise of our own busy little minds, opening them up so that the whispers of God's "still small voice"[72] may be discerned deep in our hearts, even if at a level below the threshold of our mental awareness.

Christians have been seeking silence ever since the first Desert Fathers and Mothers abandoned the cities of the Roman Empire in the early centuries of Church history. In the desert, far removed from the noise of urban life or the distractions of unnecessary possessions or social entanglements, the earliest Christian mystics drank deeply of silence, breaking it only with their recited psalms as they performed the menial tasks necessary for their livelihood.

Few of us have the luxury of that degree of silence in our lives, however; and we may assume that we are not called to immerse ourselves that deeply in absolute silence (although, even today, some hardy souls do sense such a heroic call).[73] For most of us, the core practice of Christian contemplation—the prayer of silence—involves two related tasks: seeking to foster an overall simplification of life, recognizing that, to foster the spirituality of contemplation, less noise is better than more; and engaging in a regular daily practice of resting in silent prayer.

Simplification of life and lessening the noise within it will, of course, be an individual task that may vary considerably for different people. For an older individual or even a couple with no children at home, this may be as radical as allowing their home, at least for portions of the day, to be as silent as a library or a monastery. Younger folks engaged in the midst of the joys and challenges of raising a family may do well simply to refrain from turning on the television or computer first thing in the morning, in order to allow even twenty minutes of quiet to nurture the new day.

The point behind a simpler, quieter life (externally) is to help foster the growth of *inner* simplicity and silence. Thus it would be foolish to adopt a kind of rigid insistence on observing arbitrary rules about external silence—for example, insisting that your entire household give up watching television every night after six p.m. and all day

Sunday, even though I personally think that sounds like heaven. Trying to enforce that on others who do not willingly embrace it will be about as successful as any other attempt to legislate morality, like 1920s-era Prohibition. You would be equally mistaken, however, to assume that, because it is interior silence that really matters, the quality or degree of external auditory stimulation (read: noise) is irrelevant to the pursuit of contemplation. The ideal for most people may be to seek out intuitive and gentle ways to turn away from the constant buzz of our entertainment and technological culture, instead embracing times and places of noiselessness whenever possible.

Often this means engaging in old fashioned self-discipline. I have to be careful not to sit down to my computer first thing in the morning. If I start writing before I pray, often the prayer never happens. But when I remember to pray first, I always find the time to write as well. It also means paying attention to our natural rhythms and learning to identify, support, and strengthen those times of day when we are most naturally or easily silent.

Incidentally, simplification of life can also mean seeking out fewer possessions, less clutter, fewer appointments, fewer online commitments, and less junk food, as well as making more of an effort at recycling, spending time outdoors or in nature, tending a garden, preparing wholesome food, learning or playing a musical instrument, and other simple, creative, life-enhancing activities.

The beauty behind simplifying life and cultivating silence is that it improves the overall quality of life. Moreover, it lays the foundation for the crown jewel of mystical spirituality—the regular practice of silent prayer. While there are a variety of wonderful schools of thought regarding silent prayer, let me offer a simple set of instructions that can help anyone begin to taste the pleasures of contemplative practice in a disciplined, practical way.

If at all possible, ensure that you have a period of time set aside for *uninterrupted* silence. Ask family members and housemates not to disturb you unless a true emergency arises; turn off the computer and mobile devices; silence your cell phone, TV, radio, other sound-generating gadgets.

It is important to tend to your body. We pray most fully when the totality of our being is present to the prayer. While it may be your mind that is paying attention to the subtleties of silence and listening for the silent call of the mystery, your body participates in prayer by maintaining a relaxed but poised posture, with your spine straight and erect,[74] your arms and legs positioned comfortably to remain still for the duration of the prayer, and your head above your shoulders in a position of calm alertness, neither anxiously rigid nor relaxed to the point of carelessness. If you have been exposed to non-Christian meditation practices like Zen, you will know about the use of cushions and sitting on the floor in a lotus or half-lotus position (or even just with your legs gently crossed). While this posture is indeed ideal for spending long periods in silence, there is nothing sacred or magical about it; finding a comfortable chair and sitting with both feet on the ground and your spine relaxed but erect can be just as effective.

Once you find a comfortable but sustainable posture—in other words, once you have disposed your *body* to silent prayer—you then perform the crucial task of disposing your *mind* to the silence. The challenge here is that few, if any, of us who grew up in Western Christian society have learned anything about disciplining our minds. (I use the word *discipline* not in the sense of punishing, but in the sense of training). Jesus's followers were called *disciples*, implying that discipline is an essential part of the Christian wisdom tradition. Yet, with the possible exception of personal morality, few people associate any kind of discipline with the pursuit of Christian wisdom in our day. This is unfortunate, for the fullness of a Christian discipline (training/practice) includes not only the ethics of living a good life but also the commitment to foster the gift of God's love in our lives—which, in turn, implies the cultivation of a gentle, relaxed, interior silence as the foundation of our longing, our beholding, and our intimacy with God.

Most people understand the role of discipline when it comes to physical health. We can see the sad results of how undisciplined our society is in this regard—rising rates of obesity, diabetes, and diseases related to poor nutrition or lack of adequate exercise. Discipline in our eating, sleeping, and daily exercise is essential for physical well-being. We don't need to be star athletes or eat only raw foods in order to be disciplined—people like that are going the extra mile. But all of us do need some basic discipline in caring for our bodies.

It is easy to see how our cultural tendency to avoid discipline also has a negative impact on our minds. We are mentally obese, our minds heavy with distracting and unproductive thoughts, overfed by a media that thrives on celebrity gossip, political scandal, interminable commentary (much of it inane or designed to foment strife), and the endless cycles of music, television, and movies designed to entertain (thrill or titillate), but not necessarily to nourish us. We suffer from what a friend of mine thirty years ago called "the materialism of infor-mation"—and he was speaking years before the arrival of the Internet and smart phones. We stuff our minds with junk information just as we've stuffed our bodies with junk food, and the results are, frankly, similar. So when it comes to disposing our minds to silent prayer, we have our work cut out for us.

How do we find the correct posture for the mind in silence? The key here is to give the mind something to allow it to relax but remain poised—a key point of focus where you can rest your attention and to where you can return it after it wanders, as it will inevitably do. Although such a focal point can be external (like focusing your gaze on an icon or a candle, or resting your mind in the serene chanting of monks at prayer), the two most recommended points of focus have traditionally been the breath and a short word or phrase repeated as a type of prayer.

Resting your attention on your breath makes wonderful sense both practically and spiritually. Practically, attending to your breath means entraining both mind *and* body to rest in calm attentiveness. Spiritually, the breath has direct Biblical links to all three persons of the Holy Trinity. In the Genesis creation story, God is described as breathing life into the first human being (Genesis 1:7), while Jesus uses his breath as a way of describing the gift of the Holy Spirit to the disciples (John 20:22). It's interesting to note that, in both Hebrew (*ruach*) and Greek (*pneuma*), "breath" and "spirit" are marked by the same word. To breathe is an embodied way to recall our relationship to the spirit of God.

While simply resting attentively to the breath can be a profound way to dispose ourselves to the silence of the mystery of God, many people may find that the prayerful recitation of a short word or phrase is helpful, or even necessary, to rest in the silence. Again, this has deep roots in the Christian tradition. John Cassian, a pioneer of European monasticism who spent almost twenty years studying with the Desert Fathers and Mothers, advocated the prayerful repetition of one particular verse in the Bible: "Be pleased, O God, to deliver me; O LORD, make haste to help me!" (Psalm 70:1). For Cassian, this humble prayer of supplication was the perfect prayer, and ideally suited for those who wished to pray without ceasing—to make prayer as natural, normal, and constant a part of life as breathing.

Of course, there is nothing magical or sacrosanct about that particular Bible verse, beautiful as it is; other advocates of contemplative prayer have offered different verses (or combinations of verses). The following formulation became widely accepted among Christians of the East: "Lord Jesus Christ, Son of God, have mercy on me." While not based on any one verse from the Bible, the elements of this prayer are found throughout the New Testament (see Luke 18:38, for example). This simple prayer is known as the "Prayer of the Heart" or the

"Jesus Prayer," and has long been recognized as the heart of Eastern Orthodox mystical spirituality.

It's easy to see how a prayer like the Prayer of the Heart can be combined with attentiveness to your breath to form a powerful way to enter into contemplative silence. Find your restful yet alert posture and settle in to a normal rhythm of breathing, neither too shallow nor too deep. As you breathe in, pray silently the words "Lord Jesus Christ." As you pause between inhalation and exhalation, say "Son of God." And as you breathe out, say "Have mercy on me." A common variation of the Jesus Prayer ends with "have mercy on me, a sinner." I don't particularly encourage the use of the words *a sinner*, not because we aren't sinners—we all are—but because it places too much attention on the self, rather than on God. The purpose of contemplative prayer is to lose ourselves in God, not to reinforce our self-identity in either a positive or negative way.

Incidentally, the Russian mystical treatise *The Way of a Pilgrim* explains why this prayer is known as the Prayer of the Heart. The continual repetition of the Jesus Prayer, especially entrained to the breath, moves it beyond a merely cognitive, mental function and allows it to be literally *embodied* within not just the mind but the heart as well. Because the heart is both the physical and emotional center of the body, this unity of mind and body is experienced as prayer literally emanating from the heart, as much as (or even more so) than the mind.

While both Cassian's prayer and the Prayer of the Heart are rich ways of entering into contemplative silence, others in the tradition have advocated an even simpler prayer—a prayer of just one word, slowly and mindfully repeated as the focus of attention. This word can be long (*Marantha*, as recommended by the twentieth-century Benedictine teacher John Main), or monosyllabic (the fourteenth-century mystical masterpiece *The Cloud of Unknowing* suggests using a word as simple as God). Centering prayer, the popular method of silent prayer based on the teachings of Trappist monks Basil Pennington, Thomas Keating, and William Meninger, involves using a prayer word of your choice. The idea behind reciting one single prayer word is to give the thinking mind as little stimulation as possible, instead offering one single point of focus that can be repeated lovingly and prayerfully as you embrace the silence.

Whether you choose to follow your breath in pure silence, recite a single prayer word, or use a longer prayer like the Jesus Prayer, the intent is the same—not to empty the mind, but rather to focus it. It is as impossible to empty your mind of thoughts as it is to empty your heart of beating. The invitation in silent prayer is to return continually to awareness of the silence in which the presence of God is concealed. This, indeed, is the heart of the hidden quality of mystical spirituality. Remember, *mystic* is a word that essentially means hidden. Sometimes, we human beings are graced with a powerful recognition of the presence of God in our lives; but often, we stumble through life without such a reassuring sense. Some people never feel the presence of God. But God is not an object to be grasped, so the mystical tradition assures us that silent prayer is the key to contemplation regardless of whether we sense God's presence or must rely on faith that the Divine mystery remains hidden deeply within the silence.

Let's remember John of the Cross's wonderful maxim: "Seek in reading and you will find in meditation; knock in prayer and it will be opened to you in contemplation." Christian spirituality requires a balanced diet of the kataphatic practices of sacred reading, meditation, and prayer—that leads into the apophatic practice of contemplation. These practices, taken together, provide us with all the spiritual nutrients we need to foster our capacity for beholding God and for allowing God to transform our lives.

One more practical question remains. How much time should we invest in *lectio divina* and silent contemplation? There is no hard rule here. The teachers of centering prayer suggest twenty minutes twice a day. Assuming that such silent prayer comes after the *lectio* process of reading, meditation, and prayer, a half hour for the entire practice seems minimal. If your schedule permits, this can be a wonderful and rewarding discipline. But beginners, especially, can find the thought of investing that much time in silence to be daunting; and depending on the overall nature of your family and work commitments, such a daily commitment may simply be impractical. What may work well for retirees is out of the question for a young growing family. I think newcomers to spiritual practice are best advised to focus on creating a daily habit rather than worrying about how much time is (or isn't) given to prayer. Three to five minutes given to silence, every day, will take you farther in prayer than an occasional twenty minutes here and forty minutes there. If you engage in a daily practice of silent prayer, you will soon hunger for more, so you can grow into a deeper practice as you are ready. Your heart will guide you to what is enough.

Into the Emptiness

The Trappist monk Michael Casey describes contemplation like this:

> It is a change of consciousness marked by two elements. On the one hand, there is a recession from ordinary sensate and intellectual awareness and all the concerns and programs that depend upon it. At the same time, more subtly, it is being possessed by the reality and mystery of God. Having emptied oneself in imitation of Christ (Philippians 2:7), one is filled with the fullness of God.[75]

Casey's words point to an important dimension of the mystical path that will increasingly come into play in the life of anyone who embraces contemplation. When Casey mentions "having emptied oneself in imitation of Christ," he is pointing to kenosis—a Greek word that means emptiness, but that also carries connotations of vanity, foolishness, even futility.

This is not just any kind of emptiness, however. Mystically speaking, kenosis refers primarily to Christ divesting himself of his Divinity in order to become human. In Philippians 2, Paul describes Jesus as "emptying himself" of his Divinity, his Godhood, to take on the form of a human being, a slave of matter and time. But that's not all. As we go deeper into contemplation, we find that kenosis isn't just for Christ; it's a spiritual path that all who hunger for the love of God will eventually be asked to follow. It's about as counterintuitive a concept as you can imagine, and yet it is the key—not merely to the contemplative call but indeed to the entire wisdom tradition of Jesus, the mystery of Christ.

Nature abhors a vacuum. Perhaps we can say the same thing about God. Indeed, the fifteenth-century German monk Thomas à Kempis said: "The Lord gives his blessing where he finds the vessels empty."[76]

When Christ emptied himself, pouring his Divinity out upon all things, sending first himself as a finite human being and then his Holy Spirit to those who love him, something surprising happened. The journey down (the emptying) became a journey up and out (up into love, out toward all people and things). Christ emptied himself, and humbled himself, and died a horrible death. And then God lifted him up. Into the vacuum that Christ had become, God poured the fullness of God's own love and life. Christ abandoned his own Godhood, to the point of crying out in fear and forsakenness as he suffered slow, painful asphyxiation on the cross. Total emptiness, abject humility. And into that emptiness God poured God's love. Not necessarily so that Christ could perceive it—I think we can make the case that Christ died far more conscious of his emptiness than of his Godhood. But that's the point, isn't it? In Christ's emptiness, his Divinity emerges.

Can we do the same thing? Can we empty ourselves to the point where God pours his own Divinity, his Holy Spirit into us? God, poured into our humble, human, material, earthly selves? Here we begin to get a sense of the path of contemplation—the path we are called to follow.

Please understand: kenosis is not just this year's cool spiritual trend. Kenosis is *mystical*. By its very nature, it is imbued with mystery. It is hidden, obscure, behind the scenes. It's a workhorse, not a show-horse. God didn't issue a press release to tell the cosmos: "Okay, I'm going to self-empty myself now and take on human form, to be obedient even to death." That's not how it works.

The letter of Paul to the Philippians was probably written somewhere around thirty years after the crucifixion of Jesus. See Philippians 2:5–11[77] to read about kenosis as it is presented in this letter. Thirty years is plenty of time for Paul and the other apostles to pray about what happened, and to begin to discern how the spirit of God was at work even in something as horrific as an innocent person undergoing cruel punishment at the hands of an oppressive government. To this day, Christians still struggle to make sense out of the apparently meaningless, senseless act of Jesus's execution. How raw it must have been in Paul's day, when so many members of the community had lived through the events as they happened and still carried the memories of horror and anger and fear, even after the kenosis unfolded itself into the miracle of the empty tomb.

Paul wrote about Jesus's self-emptying not long after the fact, but after the fact nonetheless. I believe this points to an important fact that remains relevant for us today: kenosis is only visible in hindsight. I think we can go as far as to say that this holy charism (Divine gift) is hidden from everyone—even from the person living the kenotic life. In other words, if you wake up one morning and say, "I think I will empty myself today," even if you spend the day performing very worthy and loving actions designed to foster your humility or lessen your dualistic mind or sense of self-importance, in truth you will still in some way miss the kenotic mark, because all of your actions will still carry the faint imprint of self-directed, self-important striving. *I* will humble *myself*—see where the emphasis is placed? "It's all about me" is the best way to distract yourself from the kenotic call.

I was tempted to write that self-focus is the opposite of kenosis, but even that would be a bit of a distortion. For kenosis is not opposite anything; it simply hides beneath all things, silently and subtly inviting us into self-forgetfulness at all times and in all circumstances. That's the beauty of it. We can answer this call to holy emptiness at any time, even when life seems to be the most wounded, the most screwed up, the most bound up in pain and suffering. Perhaps the more off-kilter our lives, the easier it is for us to do our hidden (un-self-conscious) work or radical emptying, breathing space into our suffering and inviting us to new possibilities. "I give thanks to God for every drink I took," a person in recovery once told me. "Because it took precisely that many drinks in order for me to bottom out, and that had to happen before I could get sober." Only in his most miserable, broken moment was my friend able to accept the gift of self-emptying.

The mystics have long recognized that holy emptying represents a particularly blessed gift for a lover of God. "I would say that [a person] is blessed and holy to whom it is given to experience something of this sort," wrote Bernard of Clairvaux, "so rare in life, even if it be but once and for the space of a moment. To lose yourself, as if you no longer existed, to cease completely to experience yourself, to reduce yourself to nothing is not a human sentiment but a divine experience."[78]

Kenosis is like the angels. In fact, I rather suspect that there is an Angel of Kenosis hovering over each one of us, ever present and ever willing to offer help and guidance, but only when we are ready for it—when we ask for it (consciously or sub-consciously), when we are open to receiving the gift without trying to bend it to our self-seeking will. It is said that the angels are polite, and that they never intervene in our lives if we do not want and actually ask for their help. The hidden (mystical) gift of kenosis works the same way. The invitation to self-emptying is never something that God forces on us—not just because God is so kind, but even more so because it would be against the nature of kenosis to impose it.

This is why human-engineered programs to enforce public morality (think again, for example, of the Prohibition-era efforts to eradicate alcohol consumption) typically fail. You can't make others lovingly and willingly surrender their self-will; in fact, if one person tries to force another to behave according to an arbitrary system of morality, perhaps the holiest thing that the second person can do is gently to resist the imposition.

This is what Jesus did when he blithely broke the Sabbath laws. His point was very simple: Sabbath laws are meant to be an invitation to something very much like kenosis—to a kind of spiritual self-emptying that can come about from surrendering the anxiety (or greed) that can keep us working constantly. Remember the qualities of vanity and foolishness that are part of kenosis. To a workaholic, taking one day off a week seems foolish. But underneath that contempt of the foolish lies a deeper, at best semi-conscious, fear of not having enough, which is the real driver of compulsive work.

The Sabbath laws are an invitation to let go, to self-empty, to find space for God by surrendering the controlling/fearful desire to be your own "god" of work and money. But by Jesus's day, this invitation to holy rest had become a bureaucratic system of rules governing what work was considered permissible on the Sabbath. As soon as this invitation to spiritual self-emptying became legislated into a rigid legal code in which people with power used the rules to impose limitations on those without power, it lost whatever spiritual authority it originally had and became just another legalistic form of civil and spiritual oppression. In other words, the godly call to letting-go became an *un*godly system of rules that could be used to attack and punish the "rule breakers."

It's one thing for those who already have their basic needs met to surrender striving one day a week in an act of voluntary self-emptying. But if those same people then use a legalistic understanding of the Sabbath to attack those who are poor or hungry and who, *out of their*

Answering the Contemplative Call

pre-existing kenotic humility, ignore the "rules" and gather food on the Sabbath day—that is an example of how something intended for spiritual awakening can become perverted into a type of spiritual oppression.

All this is to say that the mystical act of kenosis—of self-emptying, of freely choosing humility, of letting go of any desire to own or control God or otherwise reduce God to the level of spiritual experience—can never be systematized or encoded or reduced to a set of laws or rules or principles. We can only enter into kenosis willingly; it can never be forced on us legalistically.

The Christian mystery began with Christ's emptying of his own Divinity into the relative darkness of unknowing human experience. Christ's kenosis is the threshold to the mysteries. When we embrace our own self-emptying, we find that same threshold within ourselves. Like all aspects of the mystical path, kenosis is far more than just another spiritual experience. It's not about the experience of humility, or letting-go, or self-emptying, even though these experiences may be significant, deeply transformational, and could well be part of a truly kenotic life. But trying to squeeze holy emptiness into human experience is like trying to comprehend God with a human mind. Let it go! A much more useful approach would be to regard kenosis as an antidote to the lust for experience.

Kenosis also points to something other than a simplistic imitation of God or Christ. That's not to say that we shouldn't look to Christ for inspiration and as an example of how to conduct our lives; of course Christ can bless us in this way. But when Michael Casey used the phrase "in imitation of Christ," he was talking about kenosis itself, not about trying to act like Jesus. The key to the mystical life is less about *imitating* Christ and more about *intimacy* with him. When I met my wife, Fran, and realized that I loved her, I did not start imitating her, nor did she bother to imitate me. And this is a good thing, for I loved her for being herself, and would have found it weird if suddenly she had given up her own interests and inclinations and begun to think as I did—read the same books, listened to all the same music, dressed the same, and so forth. Our love is founded upon intimacy, not imitation.

In intimacy, we give ourselves to each other, so intimacy is a form of kenosis, of self-emptying. I empty myself of my fears and angers and loneliness to create the self-forgetful space within me where my love for Fran can emerge. And she does the same for me. That's how love flows between us—out of our humility, our emptiness. If we were busy trying to imitate each other, we would be more focused on ourselves (and whether we were doing a good enough job of imitating) than on each other. Instead of the emptiness of kenotic love, we would be starved by the obsessive/compulsive nature of self-involved posturing. If we were too busy imitating each other, we wouldn't have the time (or space) for love to flow between us.

This is, I believe, an important point to consider in our quest for the love of God, for responding to the contemplative call. Let go of any impulse to give yourself a heavenly makeover in imitation of God or of Christ. Sure, look to God, look to Christ, for inspiration in your own spiritual and ethical growth. Focus your beholding on God, not on yourself. Seek to love Christ by paying more attention to him than to yourself. Empty yourself to create the space for God's love to pour into you. When God pours love into you, God is also pouring *Divinity* into you. This is what the Fathers of the Church called *theosis*, a Greek word meaning "deification" or "divinization." This is where the mystical path leads us: not necessarily toward awesome experiences (although they may or may not happen), or even toward a sense of union with God (it may take place below the threshold of our awareness)—but always toward a life filled and transformed by love.

Here's one final thought. At the risk of contradicting Michael Casey, I suggest that, when we seek the gift of kenosis, we are not actually imitating Christ in *his* self-emptying—at least, not completely. For one thing, we are not gods taking on human form, so our

Answering the Contemplative Call

self-emptying will always be small potatoes compared to his. No. Even when we choose humility and accept our inner emptiness, we do not imitate Christ so much as we merely pay it forward. We embrace our own emptiness to open up the space for God's love to flow in us, so that it can, in turn, flow through us to others who need it even more desperately than we do.

Kenosis Makes a Difference

To deepen our appreciation of kenosis, let's see how it sheds light on the three great mystics we first encountered in Part One. Each of these mystics can deepen our appreciation of the contemplative call—which includes the call to holy emptiness.

First, consider Thomas Aquinas. He was, by any standard, one of the most important Christians of his time—a renowned philosopher, a leading theologian, a consultant who traveled across Europe helping to settle theological disputes. He was basically at the top of his game when, on that December day in 1273, he was ushered across the threshold into mystery. And while he did not completely stop his work after that point, certainly his relationship with his writing changed. Whether or not he thought his work was great before, after his mystical encounter, he saw it as only so much straw. He was emptied of any pride or vainglory related to his theological work.

Aquinas seems to symbolize kenosis as the result of a specific moment of awakening—a profound emptying as a natural consequence of a life-altering encounter with God. I do not mean to imply that he had not been humble or even empty prior to his mystical vision. Certainly, however, the encounter led to a more profound emptiness—deep enough to change his assessment of his own writing.

On to our second great mystic: Julian of Norwich. If Aquinas appears to have undergone kenosis as a consequence of a mystical event in his life, Julian appears to have received her mystical visions after having previously chosen a remarkably kenotic life. We know from her writings that, before the dramatic night in which her showings took place, she was a pious woman—a woman of prayer who prayed to know Christ's passion as fully as she could, and who prayed for what she called the "three wounds" of true contrition, compassion, and the willful longing to God.[79] In other words, she wanted to be "opened up"—for a wound is an opening, a breach in our defenses—by authentic sorrow for her misdeeds, genuine love for others, and heartfelt longing for God.

Sorrow, love, and longing—fairly mainstream religious notions, of course. What is fascinating, however, is that Julian desires for these qualities to be wounds. She does not want merely to *contain* a spirit of sorrow, compassion, and longing; she wants to *pour out* these qualities toward God, toward others, and toward the universe. She prays to be a beacon of love, fully responsible for herself (including her faults), but utterly self-giving.

I find it fascinating how so much of the language people use to explore Christian spirituality is the language of sorrow for our sins. While this is a central element in Christian tradition, Julian rightly sees such contrition as only the opening act of a fully embraced life of spiritual wisdom. Contrition merely sets the stage for the true work of the mystical path—love of neighbor and love of God. I believe that, for Julian, the process of entering in to God's holy emptiness began with her "three wounds" prayer. In praying to be wounded by contrition, compassion, and longing, she in effect prayed to be emptied of anything that stood in the way of her being a beacon of love. She prayed that all interior obstacles be cleansed away by her contrition, thereby creating the space where compassion and longing could flow through her—love rippling out to a universe starving for God and, of course, back to the God from whom all love originates.

Finally, let's briefly consider Thomas Merton. His epiphany had a quality of kenosis about it as well. For, out of his sense of falling in love with "all those people," he was emptied of whatever pride or arrogance or even mere self-defining identity may have been wrapped up in his self-image as a monk—and a famous monk at that, which is quite a contradiction. For Merton, kenosis meant being emptied of his sense of being set apart or special because he was a monk. Now he found his "specialness" (his calling) by merely being one more ordinary person in the entire human race. His epiphany left him feeling more than just empty, but earthly as well—humble, ordinary, one among many. And it was out of this newfound emptiness that he was able to transform his writing ministry, turning his attention to some of the most important things he had to say—to topics not previously or usually associated with monks, like interfaith dialogue and social and political commentary.

I believe that, if we take the time to consider the life stories and the teachings of all the great mystics of the Christian tradition, we will find this key quality of kenosis pretty much everywhere we look—not always under the same name, perhaps, for Evelyn Underhill spoke of "self-simplification," while Saint Benedict (and many others) focus on humility and holiness as their ways of understanding emptying. Meister Eckhart preached on being "empty of self" as a means to coming closer to God.[80] John Ruusbroec, likewise, spoke of an "emptiness" that "empties a person of all things" in order to "unite him with God."[81] But under whatever name, kenosis is central to the mystical tradition. Christ emptied himself, and is now emptying anyone else who comes to him in love and trust.

Answering the Contemplative Call

Thus we are called to wake up, to enter silence, to behold, and to empty ourselves—or, better yet, to allow God to empty us. I keep referring back to the mystics—not only to Aquinas and Julian and Merton, but indeed to all the great mystics—for a simple reason. As we have seen, the contemplative call beckons us to more than experiential spirituality—to silence, to solitude, and to the beholding of the Divine mystery. Beautiful as that may sound, however, we are called to a place deeper than that. The call invites us to the life of wisdom. Choosing wakefulness over slumber, silence over noise, beholding over distraction, self-emptying over self-aggrandizement, love over rage or fear—these are all pointers toward wisdom. Not knowledge, necessarily; for it is possible to stuff our brains full of facts and ideas about such qualities as love and compassion without changing our lives one bit. We can have the keenest, most informed minds on the planet, but if we do not actually *live* according to the principles of our knowledge, it does us no good. Wisdom is that beautiful place where insight and action come together—where we not only know what is good and true and beautiful, but actually live it.

Kenosis makes a difference. Themes like humility, emptiness, surrender, and sacrifice recur again and again in the writings of the great mystics because of this simple fact. The contemplative life is not about self-contempt, or masochism, or any other form of self-directed hatred. In fact, most contemplatives would agree that excessive self-loathing is not a characteristic of humility or emptiness, but actually an inverted form of pride, because it is a strategy for keeping our attention focused on the self rather than on God. So when the mystics speak of humility and kenosis, they are speaking of something much more powerful than inverse pride. They are speaking of a radical, amazing act of creating the space within your heart to allow the Holy Spirit the freedom to bring transformation, healing, and endless new possibilities into your life.

God is a God of love; therefore, God is a God of possibility. Indeed, more than once the Bible declares that with God, all things are possible.[82] For contemplatives, the infinite possibilities of Divine love represent the always-new promise of a life filled with joy, purpose, and meaning, even in the face of loss, suffering, illness, or death. Really, the only obstacle to the freedom and joy that comes from God is our own selves! Consciously or unconsciously, we mortals get in our own way, and we get in God's way. Kenosis, therefore, is an invitation to freedom—to getting out of our own way and getting out of God's way in order to create the space within us for the transforming, healing, loving, creative activity of the Holy Spirit to be born within us.

Such activity does not promise us a life of carefree bliss. God's presence in our lives is not a shortcut to endless happiness or to a problem-free existence. Indeed, if anything, the contemplative life offers a new dimension of sorrow and suffering, for to the extent that our hearts are united with God, we will be that much more sensitive to the brokenness, pain, and suffering of all God's children—of all beings. That may sound overwhelming, but the union with God that arises from kenosis means that we will never be left alone—not in our suffering, not in facing the sadness and sorrow of the world. The kenotic life will not erase suffering, but it will allow us to bear it in the deeply healing presence of Divine love, always hidden deep within us, in the heart of *le point vierge*.

This, then, is the promise and possibility of the mystical path—to hold and be held by God, who is always present whether hidden from us or not. It is the presence of God that kenosis makes available to us. And it is that loving presence that truly, finally, makes all the difference in our lives—filling us with purpose, meaning, and joy.

Where Does the Path Lead?

We have considered how the call to contemplative spirituality comes to us from God and is often recognized as a sense of longing, or even a type of inner awakening. Using the metaphor of a journey or a path to follow, we considered the steps necessary to prepare for such a pilgrimage: becoming familiar with the wisdom of those who preceded us; establishing relationships with others who share a similar sense of calling; and learning the language of silence and devotion. Finally, we looked at the first steps on the mystical path, including beholding God both as the human Christ and as the ineffable triune mystery, balancing communal worship with solitary prayer, feasting on the scripture through the prayerful process of *lectio divina,* meditating on the mysteries of the faith and how they impact our lives, and learning to rest in God's hidden presence through the practice of silent prayer—all of which lead to the mystery of kenosis, or being emptied of ourselves so that the love of God may flow to and through us.

While it sounds like a lot, these really are just the first steps on the mystical path. This is a journey that lasts a lifetime—and beyond. The spiritual life challenges us to recognize that transformation in Christ—learning to be, and to live, in the love of God—is what Eugene Peterson described as "a long obedience in the same direction." Obedience, here, needs to be understood, not in the hierarchical sense of "taking orders without question," but in a more holistic, authentic sense of deeply and profoundly *listening*—listening to God's call in our lives; acknowledging the ways in which the wisdom and insights of others on the path both nurture and challenge us; and recognizing the silence that functions like a cloud of unknowing, through which we may love but can never fully comprehend God. The listening obedience takes us in a direction—the mystical path, the path toward love and healing and an austerely abundant life. But it is a long process indeed to walk this path and to listen as we go.

There is so much more to say. Perhaps for this final chapter, it will be best to let a few of the mystics speak for themselves, offering a smorgasbord of thoughts that may be useful for you as you proceed along this path of mystery.

"Go forth and eat nothing until you get a soul friend, for anyone without a soul friend is like a body without a head."[83] The ancient Irish saint Brigit of Kildare gave this succinct advice to a young seeker who came to her for a word of guidance. Of course, I emphasized the importance of spiritual friendship in Part Two of this book; I bring it up again here simply to highlight once more how important relationships and community are to the ongoing journey. We never outgrow the need for a soul friend, just as we never outgrow the need for community.

For Christian contemplatives, community typically takes at least three forms. First, there is the community of two—what Brigit refers to in her comment as a "soul friend." In this type of spiritually intimate relationship, you have the opportunity to disclose the most hidden

stirrings of your true spiritual heart to another. This can be a very informal kind of friendship—two people who share their experience of
prayer with one another, as peers in faith—or it can be a more formal
relationship with a teacher or an elder, a "spiritual director"—someone devoted to the study and practice of contemplative spirituality
who shares insights and wisdom with others.

The second form of community is the larger community of faith
where we grow in the art of loving others for the sake of Christ. Traditionally, the monastery or convent functioned in this way for cloistered
contemplatives. For those of us who live outside monastic walls, our
local churches, or a house Church, or a monastic lay associate community, or even a meaningful ministry organization like a twelve-step
group can fulfill this function.

Finally, there is the community of the world, where we learn to
see all people as our brothers and sisters—even those who do not
share our faith, or who do not think or vote as we do, or look like
we do. God can use anyone and everyone to teach us how to give and
receive love. For true contemplatives, the entire world is our community. When Thomas Merton received his epiphany, *everyone* he saw—
not just monks or Catholics—was "shining like the sun." As Thérèse of
Lisieux observed: "Let us love, since that is all our hearts were made
for."[84] Likewise, Teresa of Avila said: "The Lord doesn't look so much at
the greatness of our works as at the love with which they are done."[85]

"God is love, and those who abide in love abide in God, and God
abides in them" (I John 4:16). Therefore, love really is central to the
mystical life. Bernard of Clairvaux insisted: "The capacity of any man's
soul is judged by the amount of love he possesses; hence he who loves
much is great, he who loves a little is small, he who has no love is
nothing."[86] Teresa of Avila echoes him when she notes "that true perfection consists in love of God and neighbor . . . This mutual love is
so important that I would never want it forgotten."[87] The Orthodox
mystic Maximus the Confessor related love to the splendor of heavenly

beings: "The unutterable peace of the holy angels is attained by these two dispositions: love for God and love for one another."[88] Meanwhile, the great theologian (and mystic) Augustine of Hippo reminds us that an important dimension of love is appropriate love for ourselves, and even that comes from God: "The more we love God," notes Augustine, "the more we love ourselves."[89]

All this talk about love can seem a little precious—kind of a sweet, sentimental religion, full of *kum ba yah* but not very realistic. But since "God is love," our destiny as contemplatives is to give and receive love, which is to say our destiny is to give and receive *God*. Michael Casey states it even more radically still: "Christian life consists not so much in being good as in becoming God."[90] He cites the Church Fathers to back up this audacious declaration.

Here Casey is speaking of *theosis*, or deification—in other words, becoming God. When translated from Greek to Latin, this word came to describe the much less mystical concept of *sanctification*, or becoming holy. Quite a difference! But theosis is rooted even in the Bible, as in Saint Peter's tantalizing statement that Christians are "partakers in the Divine nature" (II Peter 1:4). The Greek word translated here as "partaker" is *koinonos*, which can also be translated as "sharers," suggesting that Christians share in the nature of God.[91] Athanasius, the fourth-century bishop of Alexandria, said: "God became man so that man might become God."[92] Meister Eckhart's comment on beholding deserves to be repeated here, for it also points to *theosis*: "[T]he eye with which I see God is exactly the same eye with which God sees me. My eye and God's eye are one eye, one seeing, one knowledge and one love."

Theosis is not just a cool idea, a nifty notion given to us so that we can feel good about ourselves. The point behind theosis, behind sharing in the nature of love, is that we can bring heaven to earth and share God's love as abundantly and lavishly as God shares it with us.

I imagine that Richard Rohr had this in mind when he wrote:

Answering the Contemplative Call

This is amazing. It's as if God is saying, "All I want are some living icons out there who will communicate who I am, what I'm about and what is happening in God." . . . It is not a "those who do it right get to go to heaven" thing, as much as it is a "those who live like me are in heaven now" thing![93]

Indeed, *The Cloud of Unknowing* agrees, using language that takes us right back to the very beginning of our journey: "In fact, anyone who longs for heaven is already there in spirit. The highway to heaven is measured by desires, not by feet. Our longing is the most direct route."[94]

From longing, to awakening, to beholding, to silence, to prayer, to kenosis, to theosis. Thus begins the mystical journey. And I do mean "begins." There is far more to come. The process of transformation into holiness is long and slow. And the fact that contemplation points beyond mere sanctification to deification does not make sanctification irrelevant. In fact, for many of the mystics, the bulk of their writing and teaching consisted in instruction on how to become holy. Holiness is not something we *do* so much as it is a *state* we enter. "Do not think to found holiness upon doing; holiness must be founded upon being," said Meister Eckhart.

Works do not make us holy. It is we who must make works holy. For no matter how holy works may be, they do not make us holy because we do them, but in so far as we within ourselves are as we should be, we make holy all that we do, whether it be eating, or sleeping, or working, or what it may.[95]

Beyond even the quest for holiness (what the ancient contemplatives called *catharsis*, or purification) lies the promise of illumination. In the words of Richard of St. Victor, one of the leading mystical theologians of the Middle Ages: "It is the property of contemplation to cling with wonder to the manifestation of its joy."[96] Even that is not the end of our journey, however, for a more terrifying process of letting-go called the dark night of the soul awaits the maturing contemplative as a sort of second, or deeper, purification. Sustaining the mystical life through the ups and downs of illumination and purgation is the most unglamorous, and yet most important, of virtues—perseverance. Remember that simple wisdom: "Be gentle with yourself; change takes time."

Walter Hilton makes the following suggestion:

> Keep to whatever work or movement you experience—prayer or meditation, silence or speech, reading or listening, solitude or community, walking or sitting still—that helps you to strengthen and nourish your desire, that makes you freest from lust and the world's way of thinking, that better unifies your energies and makes you burn more with the love of God.[97]

These words of counsel imply that the alpha point of the mystical life—that mysterious longing—never fully leaves us. For herein is a paradox: contemplation means we seek the God who has already found us, but our longing will, at least on this side of eternity, never be fully satisfied.

Raimon Panikkar points out that "the progress of a spiritual person towards God is rather the progress of God in him or her. The ascent to the mountain on a person's part corresponds to the more real descent of God into his/her being."[98] True enough, but remember: this doesn't mean that we necessarily *feel* or consciously recognize this "descent of God." Even as we are transformed into partaking in the Divine nature, our sense of what is going on may never move beyond the most heart-wrenching yearning.

In the midst of that inconsolable longing, a certain kindness toward ourselves is necessary. Again, Hilton offers us advice:

> If your heart is dull and murky, and you have not much spiritual motivation but only the barest of desires and a weak will, and you would very much like to think on God but cannot; then I

hope that it will now seem good for you not to berate yourself too much, or strive within excessively, as if you would by your own might overcome your spiritual dullness.[99]

Change takes time, so be gentle with yourself.

Consider this advice from the German poet Rainer Maria Rilke: "*Live* the questions now."[100] Let the mystery of where God is calling you be open and spacious, and allow yourself to be patient as you embrace the adventure of not knowing where the contemplative call will take you. Of course, on one level we *do* know where this path will lead: to death. "No one here gets out alive," said the ill-fated rock star Jim Morrison. True enough. But if the mystical path cannot help us evade death, it can certainly transform our relationship to it.

"Learning not to fear any death, chosen or unchosen, is the truth that sets us free," says the Anglican contemplative Maggie Ross. "Death will always inspire dread, but it is the dread of a new and unknown life that is resurrection in Christ, not the kind of panic that pushes us further and further into untruth."[101]

In conclusion, here is one more insight from the Cistercian Father William of St. Thierry:

> Be wholly present to yourself, therefore, and employ yourself wholly in knowing yourself and knowing whose image you are, and likewise in discerning and understanding what you are and what you can do in him whose image you are.[102]

Here, in one simple sentence, is the heart of the contemplative call. To be present to God, begin by being present to yourself. That means remembering who you are—someone created in the image and likeness of the Divine mystery (Genesis 1:26). If only we could truly *know* who we are—images and likenesses of God, of Love, of the Creator, Redeemer, Sustainer. Be present to who you really are; remember in whose image and likeness you have been made. And suddenly, *everything* is possible (Mark 10:27). Sit in silence with that luminous, resonant truth. Behold the Mystery who loves you—and who calls you to be everything it is possible for you to be. Wake up! Your spirit shines like the sun. You have a glittering, shimmering day ahead of you. For knowing who you are, remembering who you are, and responding to your unique call—these steps are just the beginning of an adventurous journey that will last forever.

Bibliography

Aelred of Rievaulx. *The Mirror of Charity,* translated by Elizabeth Connor. Kalamazoo, MI: Cistercian Publications, 1990.

Allchin, A. M. *Participation in God: A Forgotten Strand in Anglican Tradition.* London: Darton, Longman & Todd, 1988.

Anonymous. Johnston, William, ed. *The Cloud of Unknowing and the Book of Privy Counseling.* New York: Image Books, 1973.

————. *The Cloud of Unknowing with the Book of Privy Counsel,* translated by Carmen Acevedo Butcher. Boston, MA: Shambhala, 2009.

————. *The Pilgrim's Tale* (Classics of Western Spirituality), edited with an introduction by Aleksei Pentkovsky. Mahwah, NJ: Paulist Press, 1999.

Augustine of Hippo. *Selected Writings* (Classics of Western Spirituality), translation and introduction by Mary T. Clark. Mahwah, NJ: Paulist Press, 1984.

Bourgeault, Cynthia. *Centering Prayer and Inner Awakening.* Cambridge, MA: Cowley Publications, 2004.

————. *Encountering the Wisdom Jesus: Quickening the Kingdom of Heaven Within* [audiobook]. Boulder, CO: Sounds True, 2005.

Brother Lawrence of the Resurrection. *The Practice of the Presence of God*, translated by Salvatore Sciurba. Washington, DC: ICS Publications, 1994.

Bruno Scott James (trans.). *The Letters of St. Bernard of Clairvaux*. London: Burns Oates, 1953.

————. *On the Song of Songs II*. Kalamazoo: Cistercian Publications, 1958.

Burrows, Ruth. *Guidelines for Mystical Prayer*. Denville, NJ: Dimension Books, 1976.

Casey, Michael. *Fully Human, Fully Divine: An Interactive Christology*. Liguori, MO: Liguori Publications, 2004.

————. *Sacred Reading: The Ancient Art of Lectio Divina*. Liguori, MO: Liguori Publications, 1996.

Cassian, John. *Conferences* (Classics of Western Spirituality), translated by Colm Luibheid. Mahwah, NJ: Paulist Press, 1985.

Catherine of Genoa. *Purgation and Purgatory, The Spiritual Dialogue*, translation and notes by Serge Hughes; Introduction by Benedict J. Groeschel, OFM Cap.; Preface by Catherine De Hueck Doherty. Mahwah, NJ: Paulist Press, 1979.

Chödrön, Pema. *The Places That Scare You: A Guide to Fearlessness in Difficult Times*. Boston: Shambhala Publications, 2005.

Cross, F. L. and E. A. Livingstone, eds. *The Oxford Dictionary of the Christian Church*. Oxford: Oxford University Press, 1983.

de Béthune, Pierre-François. *By Faith and Hospitality: The Monastic Tradition as a Model for Interreligious Encounter*. Leominster, UK: Gracewing, 2002.

de Caussade, Jean-Pierre. *Abandonment to Divine Providence*, translated by John Beevers. New York: Image Books, 1975.

Dillard, Annie. *Pilgrim at Tinker Creek*. New York: Harper & Row, 1974.

Eckhart, Meister. *Selected Writings*, selected and translated by Oliver Davies. London: Penguin Books, 1994.

Egan, Harvey D., ed. *An Anthology of Christian Mysticism*. Second edition. Collegeville, MN: The Liturgical Press, 1996.

Evagrius. *Evagrius Ponticus: The Praktikos and Chapters on Prayer*, translated by John Eudes Bamberger. Cistercian Studies, #4. Kalamazoo: Cistercian Publications, 1980.

Fox, George. *The Journal*. London: Penguin Books, 1998.

Fry, Timothy, OSB, ed. *RB 1980: The Rule of St. Benedict in Latin and English with Notes*. Collegeville, MN: The Liturgical Press, 1981.

Guigo II. *Ladder of Monks and Twelve Meditations*, translated with an introduction by Edmund Colledge, OSA, and James Walsh, SJ. Kalamazoo, MI: Cistercian Publications, 1979.

Hilton, Walter. *The Stairway of Perfection*, translated by M. L. Del Mastro. Garden City, NY: Image Books, 1979.

————. *Toward a Perfect Love: The Spiritual Counsel of Walter Hilton*, translated with an introduction by David L. Jeffrey. Vancouver: Regent College Publishing, 2001.

————. *Eight Chapters on Perfection and Angels' Song*, translated into modern English by Rosemary Dorward. Fairacres, Oxford: SLG Press, 1983.

Houselander, Caryll. *The Reed of God*. New York: Sheed & Ward, 1944.

Hughes, Robert Davis, III. *Beloved Dust: Tides of the Spirit in the Christian Life*. New York: Continuum, 2008.

Huxley, Aldous. *The Perennial Philosophy*. New York: Harper & Row, 1945.

Ignatius of Loyola. *Spiritual Exercises and Selected Works*, edited by George E. Ganss, SJ, et al. New York: Paulist Press, 1991.

John of the Cross. *Collected Works*. Washington, DC: ICS Publications, 1991.

Julian of Norwich. *Revelation of Love*, translated by John Skinner. New York: Image Books, 1996.

Laird, Martin. *A Sunlit Absence: Silence, Awareness, and Contemplation*. New York: Oxford University Press, 2011.

————. *Into the Silent Land: A Guide to the Christian Practice of Contemplation*. New York: Oxford University Press, 2006.

Leech, Kenneth. *Soul Friend: Spiritual Direction in the Modern World*. New revised edition. London: Darton, Longman & Todd, 1994.

————. *Subversive Orthodoxy: Traditional Faith and Radical Commitment*. Toronto: Anglican Book Centre, 1992.

————. *True Prayer: An Invitation to Christian Spirituality*. Harrisburg, PA: Morehouse, 2001.

Leloup, Jean-Yves. *Being Still: Reflections on an Ancient Mystical Tradition*, translated by M. S. Laird, OSA. Mahwah, NJ: Paulist Press, 2003.

Lewis, C. S. *Letters to Malcolm: Chiefly on Prayer*. San Diego: Harcourt Brace Jovanovich, 1964.

————. *The Lion, the Witch, and the Wardrobe*. New York: Macmillan Books, 1950.

————. *The Pilgrim's Regress*. Grand Rapids, MI: Eerdmans, 1981.

————. *The Voyage of the "Dawn Treader."* New York: Macmillan, 1952.

Maitland, Sara. *A Book of Silence*. Berkeley, CA: Counterpoint, 2009.

Marechal, Paul. *Dancing Madly Backwards: A Journey into God*. New York: Crossroad, 1982.

May, Gerald G. *Will and Spirit: A Contemplative Psychology*. San Francisco: Harper & Row, 1982.

McColman, Carl. *The Big Book of Christian Mysticism: The Essential Guide to Contemplative Spirituality*. Charlottesville, VA: Hampton Roads, 2010.

————. *The Aspiring Mystic: Practical Steps for Spiritual Seekers*. Holbrook, MA: Adams Media, 2000.

McGinn, Bernard, ed. *The Essential Writings of Christian Mysticism*. New York: Modern Library, 2006.

McNamara, William. *Earthy Mysticism: Contemplation and the Life of Passionate Presence*. New York: Crossroad, 1987.

Merton, Thomas. *Conjectures of a Guilty Bystander*. New York: Image Books, 2009.

————. *Contemplative Prayer*. New York: Image Books, 1971.

————. *New Seeds of Contemplation*. New York: New Directions, 1961.

————. *The Inner Experience: Notes on Contemplation*, edited by William H. Shannon. San Francisco: HarperSanFrancisco, 2003.

————. *Thomas Merton in Alaska*. New York: New Directions, 1988.

————. *The Seven Storey Mountain*. Garden City, NY: Image Books, 1970.

Nh'ăt Hanh, Thích. *Living Buddha, Living Christ*. New York: Riverhead Books, 1995.

Nikodimos of the Holy Mountain and Makarios of Corinth (compilers). *The Philokalia: The Complete Text* (Volumes 1–4). London: Faber and Faber, 1979, 1981, 1984, 1995.

Nouwen, Henri J. M. *The Wounded Healer: Ministry in Contemporary Society*. New York: Image Books, 1979.

———. *Bread for the Journey*. San Francisco: HarperCollins, 1997.

O'Donohue, John. *Anam Cara*. San Francisco: Harper Collins, 1997.

———. *Four Elements: Reflections on Nature*. New York: Harmony Books, 2010.

Patanjali. *The Yoga Sutras of Patanjali*. Translated and introduced by Alistair Shearer. New York: Belltower, 2002.

Patmore, Coventry. *The Rod, the Root, and the Flower*. Freeport, NY: Books for Libraries Press, 1950.

Pseudo-Dionysius. *The Complete Works* (Classics of Western Spirituality). New York: Paulist Press, 1987.

Pseudo-Macarius. *The Fifty Spiritual Homilies and the Great Letter*, translated by George A. Maloney, SJ. New York: Paulist Press, 1992.

Reinhold, H. A., ed. *The Soul Afire: Revelations of the Mystics*. Garden City, NY: Image Books, 1973.

Richard of St. Victor. *The Twelve Patriarchs, The Mystical Ark, Book Three of the Trinity* (Classics of Western Spirituality). New York: Paulist Press, 1979.

Rohr, Richard. *Everything Belongs: The Gift of Contemplative Prayer*. New York: Crossroad, 2003.

———. *The Naked Now: Learning to See as the Mystics See*. New York: Crossroad, 2009.

———. *Things Hidden: Scripture as Spirituality*. Cincinnati: St. Anthony Messenger Press, 2008.

Rollins, Peter. *How (Not) to Speak of God*. Brewster, MA: Paraclete Press, 2006.

Ross, Maggie. *The Fountain and the Furnace: The Way of Tears and Fire*. New York: Paulist Press, 1987.

————. *Pillars of Flame: Power, Priesthood, and Spiritual Maturity*. San Francisco: Harper & Row, 1988.

————. *Writing the Icon of the Heart: In Silence Beholding*. Abingdon, UK: Bible Reading Fellowship, 2011.

Russell, Norman. *The Doctrine of Deification in the Greek Patristic Tradition*. Oxford: Oxford University Press, 2004.

Ruusbroec, John. *Spiritual Espousals* (Classics of Western Spirituality). New York: Paulist Press, 1985.

Sellner, Edward C. *Stories of the Celtic Soul Friends*. Mahwah, NJ: Paulist Press, 2004.

Steere, Douglas V. *Prayer and Worship*. Richmond, IN: Friends United Press, 1978.

Teresa of Avila. *Collected Works* (Volumes 1–3). Washington, DC: ICS Publications, 1976, 1980, 1985.

————. *The Interior Castle* (Classics of Western Spirituality), translated by Kieran Kavanaugh, OCD, and Otilio Rodriguez, OCD; Preface by Raimundo Panikkar. New York: Paulist Press, 1979.

Underhill, Evelyn. *Mysticism: A Study in the Nature and Development of Spiritual Consciousness*. New York: E. P. Dutton & Co., 1961.

————. *Practical Mysticism*. New York: E. P. Dutton & Co., 1915.

————. *The Spiritual Life*. Wilton, CT: Morehouse Barlow, 1955.

William of St. Thierry. *Exposition on the Song of Songs*, translated by M. Columba Hart, OSB. Kalamazoo: Cistercian Publications, N.D.

Notes

1. Rabbi Nosson Scherman, ed., *The Stone Edition Tanach: The Artscroll Series, Student Size Edition* (Brooklyn, NY: Mesorah Publications, 2011), p. 1489. The Hebrew word *dumiyyah* in this verse has the sense of "quiet waiting"—in other words, the silence of contemplation. Sadly, many English versions of the Bible mistranslate this verse, omitting any reference to silence—a consequence, perhaps, of our culture's bias against mystical spirituality.

Introduction

2. John O'Donohue, *Anam Cara* (San Francisco: Harper Collins, 1997), pp. 89–90.
3. From the introduction to *Catherine of Genoa: Purgation and Purgatory; The Spiritual Dialogue* (New York: Paulist Press, 1979), p. xiii.
4. Ruth Burrows, *Guidelines for Mystical Prayer* (Denville, NJ: Dimension Books, 1976), p. 6.

Part One

5. Bernard of Clairvaux, *The Letters* (London: Burnes & Oates, 1958), p. 156.

6. C. S. Lewis, *The Pilgrim's Regress* (Grand Rapids, MI: Eerdmans, 1981), p. 203.

7. Teresa of Avila, *The Autobiography of St. Teresa of Avila*, translated by Kieran Kavanaugh, OCD, and Otilio Rodriguez, OCD (New York: One Spirit, 1995), p. 356.

8. Quoted in *The Soul Afire: Revelations of the Mystics,* edited by H. A. Reinhold (Garden City, NY: Image Books, 1973), p. 452.

9. Psalm 139:8; Jeremiah 23:24.

10. Thomas Merton, *New Seeds of Contemplation* (New York: New Directions Press, 1962), p. 39.

11. Evelyn Underhill, *Mysticism* (New York: E. P. Dutton, 1961), p. 176.

12. Richard Rohr, *The Naked Now: Learning to See as the Mystics See* (New York: Crossroad, 2009), pp. 18–19.

13. *Metanoia* is a Greek word that suggests adopting a new (or higher) mind—but in most English translations of the Bible, it has been rendered as "repentance," a word that has a narrowed, anemic connotation related to a moralistic renunciation of prior misdeeds. While certainly *metanoia* can entail a radical change in behavior, the original Greek word has a much richer meaning beyond what "repentance" implies.

14. Julian's visions occurred either on the eighth or the thirteenth of May, 1373. Early manuscripts, all written by hand and using Roman numerals, disagree: the date is recorded as either the VIII of May, or the XIII of May. When you consider how easily a scribe could mis-write a V for an X (or vice versa), the mistake makes sense. But since we don't know which of the written manuscripts is the earliest/most accurate, the actual date remains a mystery.

15. Thomas Merton, *Conjectures of a Guilty Bystander* (New York: Image Books, 2009), p. 155.

16. Quoted in H. A. Reinhold, *The Soul Afire*, p. 112.

17. John of the Cross, *Collected Works* (Washington, DC: ICS Publications, 1991), p. 282.
18. Evelyn Underhill, *Mysticism*, p. 176.
19. *The Cloud of Unknowing with the Book of Privy Counsel*, translated by Carmen Acevedo Butcher (Boston: Shambhala, 2009), p. 159.
20. See her autobiography, chapter 29.
21. I am profoundly indebted to the writing of Anglican solitary Maggie Ross whose work has helped me to see the crucial importance of beholding in the contemplative life. See especially her *Writing the Icon of the Heart: In Silence Beholding* (Abingdon, UK: Bible Reading Fellowship, 2011), and her blog, *www.ravenwilderness. blogspot.com*, as essential reading on the topic, not only of beholding, but also of silence.
22. Meister Eckhart, *Selected Writings,* translated by Oliver Davies (London: Penguin Classics, 1994), p. 179.
23. *Protrepticus*, 12.93, translated by G. W. Butterworth, quoted in Norman Russell, *The Doctrine of Deification in the Greek Patristic Tradition* (Oxford: Oxford University Press, 2004), pp. 33–34.

Part Two

24. Jiddu Krishnamurti, "Dissolution Speech," *www.jkrishnamurti.org/ about-krishnamurti/dissolution-speech.php.*
25. C. S. Lewis, *Letters to Malcolm* (San Diego: Harcourt, Inc., 1964), p. 65.
26. Quoted in *The Soul Afire: Revelations of the Mystics,* edited by H. A. Reinhold (Garden City, NY: Image Books, 1973), p. 424.
27. Evelyn Underhill, *Mysticism* (New York: E. P. Dutton, 1961), p. 195.
28. See Basil Pennington, *Centering Prayer,* (New York: Image Books, 1982), pp. 26–32.
29. Walter Hilton, *The Stairway of Perfection*, translated by M. L. Del Mastro (New York: Image Books, 1979), p. 115.
30. Teresa of Avila, *The Collected Works, Volume 2* (Washington, DC: ICS Publications, 1980), p. 286.

31. Julian of Norwich, *Revelation of Love*, translated by John Skinner (New York: Image Books, 1996), p. 5

32. Jean-Pierre de Caussade, *Abandonment to Divine Providence* (New York: Image Books, 1975), p. 114.

33. C. S. Lewis, *Letters to Malcolm,* p. 64.

34. Gerald G. May, *Will and Spirit* (San Francisco: Harper & Row, 1982), p. 319.

35. Kenneth Leech, *Soul Friend*, revised edition (London: Darton, Longman & Todd, 1994), p. xviii.

36. Kenneth Leech, *Soul Friend*, p. xvii.

37. Quoted in Bernard McGinn, *The Essential Writings of Christian Mysticism*, p. 332.

38. Louis Massignon, quoted by Pierre-François de Béthune, OSB, in *By Faith and Hospitality* (Leominster, UK: Gracewing, 2002), p. 16.

Part Three

39. St. Teresa of Avila, *Collected Works, Volume 2* (Washington, DC: ICS Publications, 1980), pp. 399–400.

40. Caryll Houselander, *The Reed of God* (New York: Sheed and Ward, 1944), p. 100.

41. Quoted in *The Soul Afire: Revelations of the Mystics*, edited by H. A. Reinhold (Garden City, NY: Image Books, 1973), p. 453.

42. From *The Life of Moses*, book 2, part 165, quoted in Jean-Yves Leloup, *Being Still: Reflections on an Ancient Mystical Tradition* (New York: Paulist Press, 2003), p. 51.

43. Quoted in Jean-Yves Leloup, *Being Still*, p. 56.

44. Quoted in Aldous Huxley, *The Perennial Philosophy* (New York: Harper and Brothers, 1945), p. 25.

45. Kenneth Leech, *Subversive Orthodoxy* (Toronto: Anglican Book Centre, 1992), p. 51.

46. Walter Hilton, *The Stairway of Perfection*, translated by M. L. Del Mastro (New York: Image Books, 1979), p. 131.

Answering the Contemplative Call

47. Guigo II, *Ladder of Monks and Twelve Meditations*, translated with an introduction by Edmund Colledge, OSA, and James Walsh, SJ (Kalamazoo, MI: Cistercian Publications, 1979), pp. 90–91.

48. John of the Cross, *The Sayings of Light and Love*, 100, in *The Collected Works of St. John of the Cross*, translated by Kieran Kavanaugh, OCD, and Otilio Rodriguez, OCD (Washington, DC: ICS Publications, 1991), p. 92.

49. Julian of Norwich, *Revelation of Love* (New York: Image Books, 1996), p. 68.

50. Julian of Norwich, *Revelation of Love*, p. 68.

51. Maggie Ross, *Writing the Icon of the Heart: In Silence Beholding* (Abingdon, UK: Bible Reading Fellowship, 2011), p. 14.

52. Pseudo-Macarius, *The Fifty Spiritual Homilies and the Great Letter*, translated by George Maloney, SJ (New York: Paulist Press, 1992), p. 191.

53. Consider, for example, the radical feminist assertion that "if God is male, then the male is god"—see Mary Daly, *Beyond God the Father* (Boston: Beacon Press, 1985), p. 19.

54. The limitations of academic theology, especially in relation to spirituality, was succinctly described by the Trappist author William Meninger, who said this during a lecture in Atlanta in May 2012: "Contemplation takes the journey that theology points to."

55. Douglas V. Steere, *Prayer and Worship* (Richmond, IN: Friends United Press, 1978), p. 50.

56. Kenneth Leech, *True Prayer* (Harrisburg, PA: Morehouse, 2001), p. 8.

57. Bernard of Clairvaux, quoted in *Essential Writings of Christian Mysticism*, edited by Bernard McGinn (New York: Modern Library, 2006), p. 436.

58. This comes from the title of an anthology of Karl Rahner's spiritual writings. See Karl Rahner, *The Mystical Way in Everyday Life* (Maryknoll, NY: Orbis Books, 2010).

59. This is the trap into which books like Teresa of Avila's *Interior Castle* or James Fowler's *Stages of Faith* can lead us. Whenever we encounter a "road map" of the contemplative life, it is human nature

for each of us to try to figure out where we personally stand on the map. Have we made it to the seventh mansion of the Interior Castle? Are we at Fowler's Stage 6? As tools for discernment, these models for the interior life may have their uses, but they are so fraught with the danger of reinforcing egotistic understandings of spirituality at the expense of authentic kenotic growth that many seekers are probably better off ignoring them altogether.

60. Henri J. M. Nouwen, *Bread for the Journey* (San Francisco: Harper Collins, 1997), p. 14.

61. John of the Cross, *The Sayings of Light and Love,* 158, p. 97.

62. Walter Hilton, *The Scale of Perfection*, translated by John P. H. Clark and Rosemary Dorward (New York: Paulist Press, 1991), pp. 87–88.

63. Homily XXVIII.5; quoted in Harvey D. Egan, ed., *An Anthology of Christian Mysticism* (Collegeville, MN: The Liturgical Press, 1996), p. 87.

64. Ignatius of Loyola, *Spiritual Exercises and Selected Works*, edited by George E. Ganss, SJ, et al. (New York: Paulist Press, 1991), p. 167.

65. Thomas Merton, *Thomas Merton in Alaska* (New York: New Directions, 1988), pp. 134–135.

66. Julian of Norwich, *Revelation of Love*, p. 85.

67. Walter Hilton, *Toward a Perfect Love*, translated and introduced by David L. Jeffrey (Vancouver: Regent College Publishing, 2001), p. 47.

68 Quoted in H. A. Reinhold, *The Soul Afire*, p. 426.

69. Teresa of Avila, *The Interior Castle* (New York: Image Books, 1961), pp. 89–90.

70. Thomas Merton, *Contemplative Prayer* (New York: Image Books, 1971), p. 89.

71. Evelyn Underhill, *Mysticism* (New York: E. P. Dutton, 1961), p. 300.

72. God's presence is described as a "still small voice" in I Kings 19:12 (King James Version). The more recent New Revised Standard Version translates this same phrase as "the sound of sheer silence."

73. For a fascinating account of one postmodern woman's foray into the deep silence of the remote moors of Northern England, see

Sara Maitland's *A Book of Silence* (Berkeley, CA: Counterpoint, 2008).

74. Aspiring contemplatives sometimes ask me if it is permissible to engage in silent prayer while lying down. Of course it is "permissible" in the liberty we enjoy as children of God; but it may not be the most practical of postures, as lying down fosters, not relaxed attention, but sleep!

75. Michael Casey, *Sacred Reading: The Ancient Art of Lectio Divina* (Liguori, MO: Liguori/Triumph, 1996), p. 39.

76. Quoted in H. A. Reinhold, *The Soul Afire*, p. 421.

77. It is quite possible that the "Kenosis" segment of Philippians is actually an early Christian hymn or canticle that the author of Philippians either quoted or composed.

78. Quoted in Bernard of Clairvaux, *Essential Writings of Christian Mysticism*, p. 435.

79. Julian of Norwich, *Revelation of Love*, p. 15.

80. Meister Eckhart, *Selected Writings*, translated by Oliver Davies (London: Penguin Books, 1994), p. 225.

81. John Ruusbroec, *The Spiritual Espousals and Other Works*, translated by James A. Wiseman, OSB (Mahway, NJ: Paulist Press, 1985), p. 133.

82. Matthew 19:26; Luke 1:37; Philippians 4:13.

83. Whitley Stokes, ed., *The Martyrology of Oengus the Culdee* (London: Henry Bradshaw Society, 1905), p. 65.

84. Source unknown; collected from the Internet.

85. Saint Teresa of Avila, *Collected Works, Volume 2*, p. 450.

86. Bernard of Clairvaux, *On the Song of Songs II* (Kalamazoo: Cistercian Publications, 1976), p. 83.

87. Saint Teresa of Avila, *Interior Castle*, 1:2, pp. 295–296.

88. Quoted in Harvey D. Egan, *An Anthology of Christian Mysticism*, p. 130.

89. Augustine of Hippo. *Selected Writings*, translated by Mary T. Clark (New York: Paulist Press, 1984), p. 328.

90. Michael Casey, *Fully Human, Fully Divine: An Interactive Christology* (Liguori, MO: Liguori/Triumph, 2004), p. vii.

91. *Koinonos* is also related to *koinonia*, the Greek word for "commu-nity." Christian mystical wisdom sees partaking in the Divine nature as a social/communal act.

92. *De Incarnatione*, 54, quoted in A. M. Allchin, *Participation in God: A Forgotten Strand in Anglican Tradition* (London: Darton, Longman & Todd, 1988), p. 1.

93. Richard Rohr, *Things Hidden: Scripture as Spirituality* (Cincinnati: Saint Anthony Messenger Press, 2008), p. 35.

94. *The Cloud of Unknowing with the Book of Privy Counsel*, translated by Carmen Acevedo Butcher (Boston: Shambhala, 2009), p. 137.

95. Quoted in H. A. Reinhold, *The Soul Afire*, p. 129.

96. Richard of St. Victor, *The Twelve Patriarchs, The Mystical Ark, Book Three of the Trinity* (New York: Paulist Press, 1979), chapter 4.

97. Walter Hilton, *The Stairway of Perfection*, p. 246.

98. Raimon Panikkar's preface to the Classics of Western Spirituality edition of Teresa of Avila's *Interior Castle,* p. xvii.

99. Walter Hilton, *Toward a Perfect Love*, p. 31.

100. Rainer Maria Rilke, *Letters to a Young Poet* (New York: Vintage Books, 1986), Letter Four, p. 34.

101. Maggie Ross, *The Fountain and the Furnace: The Way of Tears and Fire* (New York: Paulist Press, 1987), p. 35.

102. William of St. Thierry, *Exposition on the Song of Songs*, translated by M. Columba Hart, OSB (Kalamazoo: Cistercian Publications, N.D.), p. 53.

About the Author

Carl McColman is an author, blogger, speaker, retreat leader and spiritual director. His blog, *www.carlmccolman.com*, celebrates the mystical and contemplative dimensions of both Christian and world spirituality. He is a regular contributor to Patheos, and his writing has also appeared in the Huffington Post and Beliefnet.

He studied Christian meditation at the Shalem Institute for Spiritual Formation, and received additional training in the art of spiritual direction from the Institute for Pastoral Studies in Atlanta. He is a professed member of the Lay Cistercians of Our Lady of the Holy Spirit, a community of laypersons under the spiritual guidance of the Trappist monks of the Monastery of the Holy Spirit. As a Lay Cistercian, his spirituality is ordered toward what Walter Hilton called "the mixed life"—devoted to the practice of contemplation within the context of marriage and family, outside of a traditional monastery.

Carl is the author of twelve previous books, including *The Big Book of Christian Mysticism: The Essential Guide to Contemplative Spirituality, 366 Celt: A Year and a Day of Celtic Wisdom and Lore,* and *The Lion, the Mouse and the Dawn Treader: Spiritual Lessons from C. S. Lewis's Narnia.*

Carl lives near Stone Mountain, Georgia, with his wife and stepdaughter.

If you are interested in finding out more, please visit his speaking page at: *www.carlmccolman.com/speaking*

You can also connect with Carl here: Blog: *www.carlmccolman.com.* Twitter: *www.twitter.com/CarlMcColman.* Facebook: *www.facebook.com/CarlMcColman.*